THE BARREN CRY

An Infertility & Miscarriage Devotional

WHITNEY HENNEMAN

WESTBOW
PRESS®
A DIVISION OF THOMAS NELSON
& ZONDERVAN

WestBow Press books may be ordered through booksellers or by contacting:

WestBow Press
A Division of Thomas Nelson & Zondervan
1663 Liberty Drive
Bloomington, IN 47403
www.westbowpress.com
1 (866) 928-1240

ISBN: 978-1-9736-9114-3 (sc)
ISBN: 978-1-9736-9116-7 (hc)
ISBN: 978-1-9736-9115-0 (e)

Library of Congress Control Number: 2020908197

Print information available on the last page.

WestBow Press rev. date: 06/17/2020

In Loving Memory of Alyse Mackena
A Daughter and a Mother

My Barren Cry

My barren cry has turned to song
My bitter cup to honey
The wilderness of bitterness
Grabbed hold with all its fury

Who is this God I once knew of
Now silent and aloof
An empty womb brings utter doom
My faith demanding proof

If time would stop and walls could talk
They'd tell of tears unending
But left behind is where you'll find
This broken heart is mending

The dark of night hath wrecked my plight
Of confidence and cheer
Now I confess I've done my best
To suffer with without fear

It's Christ in me that lets me see
A hope that's everlasting
Without His Love my grief would of
Crushed all the light within me

I know for sure my life's secure
Death's curse has lost its sting
My little ones bring healing love
All hail the King of Kings

My barren cry has turned to song
My bitter cup to honey
I praise Him now and make a vow
To always share my story

Selah

Contents

WEEK 1

WEEK 2

WEEK 3

Introduction

Hello Friend,

I'm so glad you're here. *The Barren Cry* was born out of my deepest struggles in the valley of darkness, and while our stories probably look entirely different as you are dealing with infertility or miscarriage, I think the feelings we all grapple with are wholly similar. I do want to give you a disclaimer before you read about my journey. I was able to conceive two children after a four-year infertility battle and my story is interwoven into this book. While my barren wound is now healed, the scar I will forever bear is colossal. I don't want my story to bring you pain or make you feel, in any way, that I'm speaking to you with an air of superiority because I now have children. I *am* you. I *was* you. I'm writing this book to myself in the wilderness of waiting; that rejected girl who suffers endlessly in silence as she tries to grapple with a life that looks entirely different than the one she imagined. I am able to offer you a piece of me and a piece of my story because I was once broken too. Some of my greatest hope in the midst of my battle was hearing stories of women who "made it" to the other side. But I realize that as you go from month to month or even day-to-day, your emotions might dictate, *today is not the day I want to hear about how someone else got pregnant.* Feel free, if a day strikes you wrong, to jump around, but don't give up on me!

I want to address a few things before we get started. First off, I absolutely hated it when people would say "God is faithful" about the good things in their life while I was struggling because it insinuated God was not faithful to me. My Facebook scroll would display, "New house! God is so faithful" or "Got the promotion! Isn't God good?" or "Announcing the birth of our child! My God is faithful!" It gives me pause when I say throughout my story that God is faithful to me because I am not saying God is only faithful in the good or that God loves me more because we were finally able to have children. God was still faithful to me when I was barren. He was still faithful to me when my husband was sick and had heart surgery. He was still faithful to me in the midst of debilitating panic attacks. He was still faithful in the bad, and that's the message I want you to hear along with the good. He sees you, He hears you, and He loves you.

Secondly, I want you to know that this isn't a book of blind faith. When we talk about prayer and fasting, I am not saying that just because you say eight Hail Mary's, stand on one foot while holding your breath, and whisper three humble prayers that God is going to give you a child. I've heard beautiful stories of friends who had faith that God would give them a child naturally in the waiting and it came to fruition, but that's not my story. When I talk about things like "waiting on God," I am also saying that by faith, we are called to action. If someone you knew got diagnosed with breast cancer and was apathetic to treatment but said they were "waiting on the Lord" for their healing, you would say they have foolish faith. Wouldn't you? I'm not asking you to have foolish faith or couch potato faith like let's sit back and armchair quarterback your journey to children. I am saying, let's take a look at your options, in whatever that looks like for you in your story, and let's meet God halfway. James says, "faith without deeds is dead," therefore, a response to faith is required for authentication. (James 2:26) In the midst of suffering, our faith isn't the excuse we wield for retreat, but rather the courage that carries us into battle. But don't necessarily mistake inactivity for faithlessness. If God is calling you to "wait and be still," then responding to the voice of the Holy Spirit by showing restraint is absolutely demonstrating active faith. So, tie up your shoelaces, Girl! Let's get on the treadmill, put on our prayer warrior hat, and let God do the rest. Let's go!

Set Intentions Each Week During This Time of Focused Prayer

Week One: Pray healing over your body and that your womb would be opened.

Whatever your affliction is, pray specifically that the Lord would heal you of your condition. Hormonal problems, cervical issues, recurrent miscarriages, unexplained infertility, endometriosis, male factor, and the list goes on. Sarah, Rebekah, Rachel, Hannah, and Elizabeth are all great women of the Bible who suffered at the hands of barrenness. The same God who opened their wombs is still the same God who is greater than the current obstacles you face.

Week Two: Pray for strength, resolve, and endurance in your suffering.

You might be at the beginning stages of coming to terms with your infertility or a tenured veteran. Wherever you are in your journey, pray the Lord would give you the ability, peace, and grace to continue to endure your hardship.

Week Three: Pray for your future Child/Children.

Be bold in asking God for a name to pray over during this final week. I know there can be hesitancy in opening your heart to hope but give it a chance and see if He answers you. The Lord decisively gave me a name in my time of prayer and fasting. It ended up not being our child, but I still affectionately call him my "prayer baby" to this day.

Fasting (Optional): If you would like to fast during these 21 days, we followed the guidelines of the Daniel Fast. This is a partial fast or rather a more restricted vegan diet based on Daniel's mourning fast in which he sought after the Lord. It allows water and foods grown from seed, including whole grains, vegetables, and fruits. If you are acutely processing a loss, I would recommend refraining from this portion for now.

> *In those days I, Daniel, was mourning for three weeks. I ate no delicacies, no meat or wine entered my mouth, nor did I anoint myself at all, for the full three weeks. Then he [The Angel] said to me, "Fear not, Daniel, for from the first day that you set your heart to understand and humbled yourself before your God, your words have been heard, and I have come because of your words.*
>
> —Daniel 10:2-3, 12 ESV

My Story

My story isn't necessarily about infertility—the pain, the endless longing, the disappointment, and the isolation. You know that story all too well, don't you? You get it because only those who have traversed this perilous path can truly understand the gravity of its desolation. Infertility, as cruel as it can be, is also unique in the way it powerfully bonds the hearts of those who ache with barrenness or have experienced the loss of a child. It creates an exclusive sisterhood of sorts—a ragtag team of weary warriors who alone can grasp your perpetual affliction. But the height of my infertility was one of many things that brought me to the brink of despair in 2015. I can't tell you how many times my husband and I were both in and out of the hospital that year, how many life or death moments we endured, and how many times I sat in a numb daze of terror over the thought of losing my husband or never having a child and a family to call my own. Ironically enough, the "Word of the Year" we both chose for 2015 was joy—a laughable word as we wrestled with grief, depression, and anxiety as a result of a myriad of circumstances. But through the anguish of our suffering, we were compelled to discover the *joy* of our salvation in Christ.

The overarching story for me isn't purely my heartbreak of barrenness but rather the transformation of my faith. I never ever want to relive our "Year of Death" as we call it, but as arduous as it was it is also infinitely precious to me because in my utter brokenness I was made alive. In the deepest darkness I found light. Hannah's prayer recites, "The Lord brings death and makes alive; he brings down to the grave and raises up." (1 Samuel 2:6) I read this over and over in the valley of despair. It was my barren cry—my pleading with the Lord for relief, for understanding, for redemption. And I found it, Friends: the hope when all is lost and an eternal perspective when your world around you is crumbling. I found peace in the hurricane of hopelessness. I pray my journey of faith gives you courage and resolve in your search for truth as well.

So, here it is. Here is the take away from my grueling wanderings through the barren wilderness, the bottom line that changed everything and restored my faith. Ready for it?

God *is* good *despite* our circumstances.

That's it! As simple as it sounds, that one sentence drastically changed my outlook in the valley of death. It's what life really boils down to, right? The answer to our deepest and most profound questions: suffering, death, tragedy, feeling abandoned by God, and ultimately forgotten. He is continually working for our good while the torrent of pain that assails us causes us to question everything. Even when we don't feel it, He is behind the scenes working in our favor.

Let me tell you this, though; it took me a long while to get there. I was so angry and confused at the intense spiritual oppression and physical affliction we experienced. Muddling through my perception of God in the seeming punishment of my suffering was a hard space to work out my faith in, but truly is there any other way? Our faith is tested and refined in the fire—matured and seasoned in a way our untested self could not even begin to comprehend. Honestly, one of the hardest parts during my journey was realizing that even though I desperately tried to draw near to God, He felt light-years away. Though I prayed and I prayed and I cried out, I felt increasingly abandoned from the God I thought I knew so well. "My God, my God, why have you forsaken me? Why are you so far from saving me, from the words of my groaning? O my God, I cry by day, but you do not answer, and by night, but I find no rest." (Psalm 22:1-2 ESV)

My husband Lane and I, in the heaviest part of our suffering, committed to a biblical fast: 21 days of focused praying and pleading with the Lord. We did this because it was either get healing and reprieve or die. That was 2015, the year we now jokingly refer to as "The Year of Death," as I mentioned before. I don't say that with melodramatic flair. We were literally at the precipice of life or death physically and spiritually. Retrospectively, I can piece it all together: the way God's hand was moving in our lives, the way He used our pain to prompt us to pray for others and enter their journey, the empathy I have now gained for those going through similar situations, and finally the incredibly powerful way He showed up, spoke to me directly, and told me my child was coming (by her full name I might add). I saw what a powerfully underutilized tool prayer was in my life. When you ask God to show up, it might not be immediate or an answer you fully understand at the moment but hang onto your hat, because He is going to appear in an extraordinarily monumental way.

To give you insight into my background, I was raised by two loving Christian parents in a conservative Baptist household, and I vividly remember accepting the Lord into my heart at five years old. It's uncanny how I can recall beyond a shadow of a doubt the Holy Spirit speaking to my tender, childlike heart during the altar call. I grew into the strong woman that I am today and rank a three on the Enneagram (Achiever), nicknamed by friends as "The Doer," don't-let-grass-grow-beneath-my-feet Type A, etc. You get the point, right? Along with that type of personality and a Baptist upbringing is a subconscious cause and effect. Basically, I work hard and I am rewarded. So you can imagine that my relationship with God followed parallel paths. Unknowingly, I had put Him into this box of a performance-based relationship and it really tied up nicely with a perfectly coiffed "prosperity gospel" bow on top. I do good things and God honors me with blessings, which for most of my life leading up through 2014 was the case. I was successful and accomplished in almost everything I had put my mind to. I also married my college sweetheart and true soul mate. He's the real deal! OK, so fast-forward five years into our marriage and you can imagine our shock when "The Year of Death" hit; and, let me tell you, it shook us to our core.

We should have known on that wonderfully normal New Year's Day everything was about to change. The ominous foreboding of the accident set the tone for the shoes of Job we were about to fill. We even joked about the possible meaning as we were driving to the nearest emergency room and hitting our insurance deductible the first day of the year as Lane was suffering a separated shoulder from a surfing accident; but we didn't know what was coming. We woke up that beautiful sunny morning in West Palm Beach with not a care in the world. That year we began the arduous road of intensive fertility treatments after two years of trying with minimal testing and no results. I watched friend after friend tell me they were expecting and I was starting to panic. While I scheduled surgery to fix my newly discovered endometriosis, my husband simultaneously scheduled heart surgery since he had been dealing with a condition called atrial fibrillation that was becoming increasingly worse. I sit here shaking my head on why we thought two major elective surgeries two weeks apart was a good idea, but all I can chalk it up to is the naiveté of youthful invincibility.

The medical start-up company I was working for lost Medicare reimbursement for our primary diagnostic test and overnight closed its doors. Forced to fire my entire team while also losing my own job before surgery, I slowly spiraled downward into the hormonal trauma of subsequent infertility treatments. Unbeknownst to us, what we thought was going to be a quick fix to a serious problem for Lane became not just weeks or months of recovery but years. He developed PTSD from the trauma of the 8-hour surgery and painful recovery. Our severely under-realized expectations contributed to an even more tumultuous recovery. There was a great deal of pressure riding on Lane, for if the surgery failed, there were no next steps to a reasonably normal life. This was it, our last line of defense. The next missed heartbeat meant our whole world would come crashing down around us. As he began to deal with depression and anxiety post-surgery, I started experiencing massive panic attacks from the combination of fertility medication I was on and ended up in the hospital. I don't know if you have ever experienced the physical manifestations of a panic attack, but it truly feels like you are dying. It was one of the many times that year I endured the oppressive suffocation of absolute terror.

A week after his surgery, Lane called me with an underlying panic in his voice I had never heard before. As I was driving out of our neighborhood to run some errands, he calmly described symptoms of a stroke and asked that I hurry to pick him up. I could sense the fear from my usually self-assured husband emanating from the phone like a toxic vapor, and that in and of itself was unnerving. I immediately threw the car in reverse to speed back home and take him to the ER. As I was barreling down the highway trying to keep my shaking hands at bay Lane received a text from his boss that their company had been sold and a conference call would promptly ensue in order to relay which employees were being retained. Let me pause right here just for a moment. Have you ever experienced a moment in your life that was so preposterous, so heavy, so outrageous that your only inclination was uncomfortable laughing? Not like the slapstick kind of laughter but the laughing in a funeral kind of a moment. Time slowed down, sound faded, and we were so overwhelmed it almost seemed funny...almost. Here I was jobless, just out of endometriosis surgery and gearing up for a daunting gauntlet of infertility treatments, my normally happy-go-lucky husband was dealing with a separated shoulder, major PTSD and depression from his presumed "quick fix" heart surgery, and we just got sucker-punched with an emergency trip to the ER for possible stroke with a "You're probably going to lose your job too" cherry on top.

Can anyone else out there attest to the fact that when it rains, it pours? And when I say pour, I don't mean a light drizzle because we were also struck by lightning twice that year. Think less, "Whew, that one was close!" and more Clark Griswold's cat in National Lampoons Christmas Vacation. As Floridians living in the lightning capital of the US, we are not unfamiliar with the rolling thunderstorms of summer. Oddly enough, they have a comforting nostalgia on me from the bygone days of childhood summers and bring a welcome afternoon relief to the scorching heat we endure. But one time in particular, during our 21 days of fasting and prayer, we experienced firsthand the incredible ferocity of those storms and were struck by lighting *inside* our house. After coming home from work one late afternoon, I had just stepped out of the shower into my robe and was making some hot green tea in the kitchen while catching up with Lane about his day. The explosion of blinding white light and the deafening crack was so powerful it knocked me to the ground, not near any windows I might add. Snapping like a sharp rubber band on the side of my face, the electricity bolted through our kitchen and was over before we even knew what was happening. The smell of singed smoke in the walls permeated our noses as we sat there in dumb shock, trying to fathom what just took place. It nuked our house—air conditioning units, appliances, TVs, and fans—causing tens of thousands of dollars in damage. The second occurrence happened while we were on a boat a week later off the coast of Florida when a massive storm arose out of nowhere. Lightning zinged the aluminum railings on the boat as we were hunkered down inside while waiting out the powerful wind and surging waves. Our aunt and uncle joked they needed to drop us off ASAP as we were becoming a health hazard to everyone around us. You can imagine with the precarious emotional state we were in, we felt like a colorful Mexican piñata swinging aimlessly through the air waiting for the next blow and unsuccessful cycle.

The problem with the "Performance-Based God" is that it works until suffering exists and then that theory quickly begins to unravel. In my "Achiever" mindset, our pain was an indication that we had done something to somehow step outside of God's blessings. Was there undealt with sin in my life? Had I done something to displease God? There was this cataclysmic shift in my relationship with the Lord. Suddenly I wasn't sure who He was, how I related, and I was so incredibly angry at Him, which in and of itself felt sacrilegious and shameful. Here was my husband, a 30-year-old man, arguably at the peak of his manhood and then *wham*, his health and job were in jeopardy and his identity as a man was in question. He couldn't work out, swing a golf club, or even climb a flight of stairs without passing out—even months after his surgery. Whatever he wanted to do in life he had excelled at, but now he was facing this potentially sedentary lifestyle, which for him was not a life at all. How would he take care of his family and what would the rest of his life look like? He felt every bit of his humanity and fragility. Lane told me years later he wasn't even sure he was ready to have children while I was moving forward with infertility treatments because of the state he was in.

I, likewise, had my identity shaken as a woman. My maternal instincts ran deep and the feeling that I wasn't capable of doing what my body was created for was soul-shattering. The joy of pregnancy, kids noisily running around the house, school plays, things I had never even questioned being a possibility were now an elusive dream in a nightmare reality. I was also becoming increasingly isolated as I abruptly couldn't relate to any of my friends. They had effortlessly sailed on to another phase of life and I felt desperately left behind. What did it mean to be a woman? If I never had children, what would my life look like? How would I relate to others if we never progressed into that natural next step of life? I tried to harden my heart and say I would be fine, that Lane and I could continue traveling, working, and focusing on ourselves, but deep down I knew. That baby-shaped hole in my heart was growing and my lies were only a short-lived safeguard to my one-track mind. For the first time in my life, I was failing at everything—my marriage, my job, conceiving a child, and maintaining friendships. My husband and I were on two separate life rafts floating in the open sea and one of us would occasionally glance over and give the "I'm still alive" wave. Also, the job I had poured myself into for years was gone and with it my identity as a respected medical sales manager. Our suffering that year followed parallel paths in that who we thought we were, how we identified, and our deepest longings were now suddenly stripped bare. Lane's desire and ability to care for a family coupled with my capacity to physically provide that family looked about as lively as a lonely rolling tumbleweed in those moments.

We decided to do a 21-day prayer and fast as a desperate last-ditch effort to our crushing agony. It made me angry when people would say, "God will never give you more than you can handle" because I felt entirely overwhelmed. At this point, Lane had relapsed with his atrial fibrillation and was unreachable emotionally. I had put our infertility treatments on pause after six months of failed cycles due to a humiliating in-office meltdown. No one told me an ovarian cyst was cause for a cycle cancelation! Like the sharp flick of a pin on a loaded grenade, the nurse's flippant attitude and the unexpected realization that I had to wait until the following month to try *another* IUI unleashed an explosion of emotions I didn't even know I was packing. Never did I think as a grown woman that a crowded waiting room full of anxious couples would see me sob my way out into the parking lot, but I gave quite the show. We were both in pure survival mode. I needed a sign. I needed God to show up in a big way. I desperately needed answers and so I prayed like my life depended on it.

> *In her deep anguish Hannah prayed to the*
> *Lord, weeping bitterly.* 1 Samuel 1:10

I was Hannah in the house of the Lord shouting my barren cry with all that I had left in me. And God was silent. Nothing. The eerie hollowness of my prayers bounced listlessly through the room and I have never felt further from Him. God spoke to me only once in those three weeks after I had prayed for Him to reveal a child's name to me. He gave me the name "Gift of God." A week later, I found out my pregnant cousin Alyse, who was battling an aggressive cancerous brain tumor, decided to name her son Mathias, or "Gift of God." Why Lord? Why reveal his name and not my own baby? I was so confused and conflicted but prayed obediently. Tragically my cousin, a young mother of two small children, lost her battle with cancer the day before I gave birth to my own son. Her sweet baby is now a healthy, thriving little boy who I know will go on to accomplish great things one day. Those three weeks were not what I thought they were going to be. Rather than receiving the things we prayed for, we instead endured a humbling lesson in surrender—surrender of our health, surrender of our identity, and surrender of a family. Our two options were quite simple: either trust God had a purpose for our pain or succumb to the chaos of meaningless suffering. We could have real hope in the greater story of redemption Christ offers or believe in nothing beyond the expanse this universe provides. Like the story of Jacob wrestling with God and yielding a broken hip, we wrestled with God and experienced a brokenness of spirit. (Genesis 32:22-32) The fast culminated into a final prayer in which our self-perceived control over these areas of our life had been definitively severed.

Though I felt resolve in my efforts to reach God, my once ironclad faith was seeping away with every day that passed and I received no word from Him. It had been months since we had completed our prayer and fasting. We made a decision to move forward with IVF at the beginning of 2016, mainly for insurance purposes, but also to give me a break from the emotional rat race of monthly cycles and daily doctor visits. The verse, "Children are a heritage from the Lord, offspring a reward from him." (Psalms 127:3) reverberated loudly in my head that I was indeed *not* loved by an omnipotent God. I had surely slipped through the cracks. By the prompting of my aunt and the nagging impulse that my pain had to mean something, I began the Beth Moore study of James called *Mercy Triumphs*. I leisurely went through the days, not necessarily expecting to find anything earth-shattering, until I watched the week three video on James 1:2-4, which I'm sure you've heard many times:

> *Consider it pure joy, my brothers and sisters, whenever you face trials of many kinds, because you know that the testing of your faith produces perseverance. Let perseverance finish its work so that you may be mature and complete, not lacking anything.*

She focused on the central theme of the coexistence of joy and anguish. I identified with the agony she described and how it paralleled the spiritual and physical oppression we were in the midst of. She wrapped the session up by talking about labor pains resulting in an impending symbolic birth and then looked directly into the camera for her final takeaway. I will remember her next words for the rest of my life as she pleaded with urgency: *Don't give up before the baby is due*! The ending music played softly in the background as she started praying and my body went numb. She obviously meant it in a metaphorical context but I was certain those words were my life raft from God. He was saying, "Hang in there sweet daughter. Keep pushing! Your baby is so close and I am in complete control." The realization of the message was slowly seeping into my pores and the holy awe surrounding me was palpable. God had spoken. I sat still in shock for a few moments as the slow trickle of tears burst forth into a long-awaited, healing sob. It was as if the priest in Hannah's story just told me, "Go in peace, and may the God of Israel grant you what you have asked of Him." (1 Samuel 1:17) The Lord had not spoken in hidden meanings or illusive imagery; it was as straightforward as I so desperately needed to hear. He had just promised me that my James baby (*To Replace Anguish with Joy*) was coming. For the third time that year, lightning struck, only this time it wasn't physical. I instead experienced the powerfully electric and holy presence of God.

I was in such disbelief I couldn't contain myself and made Lane watch it when he got home. I treasure that video as something far more precious than gold. It was God's private love letter to me in which He promised something I dared not even hope for and like streams of water to a weary desert traveler I drank it in. I wouldn't realize it until years after I gave birth, but Beth Moore also references the singing group Selah in the video. Not yet known to me, my sweet daughter's name was being softly whispered over me: *Selah James*. He was honoring me with the first glimpse of the dawn sun; the brilliant orange sky breathing life into the ravages the dark night had brought. The battle was almost over. Two things were born in my heart that day: a hope of life not only in the birthing whisper of motherhood but also an eternal hope where the emerging of a new-found and deeper faith in the God of all creation was born.

Infertility has made my salvation more real to me than ever. Just as I don't deserve the free gift of eternal life, I also didn't inherently deserve children any more than the barren woman next to me but God was still gracious in rescuing me from deep waters. I conceived my precious daughter in May of 2016 and gave birth to her the following February. The extraordinary redemption of a child simultaneously rebirthed the redemption of my soul and threadbare faith. My barren cry has turned to song, my bitter cup to honey, and I will sing His praises for the rest of my days.

In God we have boasted continually, and we will give thanks to your name forever. Selah

—Psalms 44:8 ESV

WEEK 1
DAY 1-7

Day 1

SOVEREIGN GOD

"And when the dew had gone up, there was on the face of the
wilderness a fine, flake-like thing, fine as frost on the ground.
When the people of Israel saw it, they said to one another,
'What is it?' For they did not know what it was. And Moses
said to them, 'It is the bread that the Lord has given you to
eat…"Now the house of Israel called its name manna. It was like
coriander seed, white, and the taste of it was like wafers made
with honey. Moses said, "This is what the Lord has commanded:
'Let an omer of it be kept throughout your generations, so
that they may see the bread with which I fed you in the
wilderness, when I brought you out of the land of Egypt.'"
Exodus 16:14-15, 31-32 ESV

Intense suffering causes us to reevaluate our faith. Has it broken
yours or made it stronger? Or are you somewhere in between? One
of the questions I found myself asking amid my struggle was: If
God is truly good and He says children are a "reward of the Lord"
(Psalm 127:3), why has He chosen not to bless me? I knew He was
involved in my story, but if He had the power to heal me and elected
not to, would I still praise Him? Would I still want to? My ultimate
conclusion was this:

Our circumstances are not the lens through which we should view God.

For, if your circumstances are good, then God is good; but if you are suffering, then God cannot be good, right? No, Sister. God is unchanging, and He is good ALL the time—despite our trials or successes. The fact is we live in a fallen, sinful world of death and destruction where our circumstances fluctuate with the seasons of life. Whether God chooses to heal our bodies or to bless us with children is an irrelevant correlation to His goodness, mercy, and power. Suffering challenges our preconceived notions of God in that it compels us to determine His true nature. C.S. Lewis lays out "the problem of pain, in its simplest form" —the paradoxical idea that "If God were good, He would wish to make His creatures perfectly happy, and if God were almighty He would be able to do what He wished. But the creatures are not happy. Therefore God lacks either goodness, or power, or both.'"[1]

So how do we reconcile our suffering with a good God who seemingly has control over our circumstances? I believe the following quote offers some insight into the broader context of our hardship:

> *God's "sovereignty" means that He is absolute in authority and unrestricted in His supremacy. Everything that happens is, at the very least, the result of God's permissive will. This holds true even if certain specific things are not what He would prefer. The right of God to allow mankind's free choices is just as necessary for true sovereignty as His ability to enact His will, wherever and however He chooses.*[2]

It always frustrated me that God placed the tree of the knowledge of good and evil in the garden of Eden in the first place. (Genesis 2:17) However, it occurred to me that for us to possess authentic freedom, the ability for choice must exist. God gave us commands and instructions on how He wants us to live, but allows us the opportunity to either obey or reject Him. The choice Adam and Eve made, therefore, have greater implications within the consequences of sin that now enter your story. That being said, there comes a point at which suffering forces us to reconcile one of two realities: a universe of order or a universe of chaos. Either we believe that God is sovereign or we must resign ourselves to meaningless suffering; and I would firmly submit we are not adrift in chaos. It's comforting to know that God's immutable qualities are such that He cannot contradict Himself and they remain true now and forevermore: "I the Lord do not change;" (Malachi 3:6) When circumstances seem out of control, we can rest assured in three concrete truths: God loves us, He is unchanging, and we are witness to undeniable order within nature (or rather, His creation). Those certainties will never fail you or me.

Just because you are in the wilderness of waiting does not mean God has relinquished control of your story. The wilderness was a sacred place for the Israelites. It was there God walked intimately with our forefathers of faith, met their most basic needs, sent manna from Heaven, performed great miracles, and prepared them for the promised land. It was also a barren, burdensome place where every day was fraught with challenges that assaulted their bodies and souls; but it is in this barren place we find ourselves that our faith is refined. It is in our need of God that our falsely perceived self-reliance is stripped away, and we are able to, maybe for the first time ever, see clearly His provision and understand His faithfulness. It is in the wilderness we learn God *is* sovereign. So don't be overtaken in your sorrow. He is still actively participating in your story, quietly pursuing you even when you cannot feel it.

After much soul searching, my answer was, "Yes." Yes, I would still trust God even if I did not receive the healing I so desperately wanted. Just as the manna God provided for the Israelites constituted enough for one day's nourishment, so His strength will also be sufficient for today in your time of desperation. Believe that your story is not yet finished; believe there is hope even if you are in the wilderness and have faith that He loves you!

Dear Lord,

Through the chaos and suffering this life has bestowed on me, I have faith you are in control and trust that you are working for my good. I rest in the knowledge you are the same God today as you were at the beginning of creation. I pray you would show up in a real way over these next 21 days. Speak to me, O God! My broken and weary heart is waiting for you. "But those who suffer he delivers in their suffering; he speaks to them in their affliction." (Job 36:15)

In Jesus' name, Amen.

Week One: *Pray healing over your body and that your womb would be opened.*

Day 2

ANXIETY

"When Anxiety was great within me, your
consolation brought me JOY."
Psalms 94:19

Is anxiety eating you alive? Not like the: "I'm worried about those
ten extra pounds," but an "I'm not sure I can physically make it
through the day" kind of feeling. You wake up and that instant hot
surge creeps into your belly, forcing you into straight-up survival
mode. The trauma of losing a child, the anxiety of conceiving again
after a miscarriage, or the hopelessness of trying month after month
with absolutely nothing to show for it—these situations can all work
you into deep-rooted anguish. "In her deep anguish Hannah prayed
to the Lord, weeping bitterly." (1 Samuel 1:10)

Did you know the Bible tells us 365 times not to fear or worry?
Easy to say, "Do not worry today, Whitney!" but hard in actual
application, especially when you are suffering from trauma,
depression, or a hormonal imbalance. Through the blood draws, and
the appointments, and the surgeries, and the needles, and the drugs,
and the hope, and the crushing disappointment, life still trudges on.
The trauma of it all can be entirely overwhelming, but time waits for
no one. Relationships still need tending, work demands deadlines,

and responsibilities await your ability to manage them. In this life-changing all-consuming darkness, it's difficult to see the light at the end of the tunnel or feel in any sense that you are further along today than you were the day before. I have been there and lived through the grueling day-to-day roller coaster infertility lends itself to. But it is in this complicated mess that God *can* still use your beautifully broken self! You are not forgotten and you are not purposeless.

I cannot stress enough how important a Christian counselor is during this season of suffering. My counselor identified with my anxiety in a way that I felt understood and normal. But my most important takeaway from those counseling sessions was her challenge to do something with my pain by serving others! At first, I was a little offended. I did not have the emotional capacity to help others; in fact, I could barely even take care of myself! It is so easy in this season to go inward—and that's justifiable—but I can promise you this, Sister, God has a purpose for your pain. So, will you also answer this same challenge I was given? My counselor is the reason Hope Infertility Support Group was born, and more importantly, why you are reading this very book. As you are crushed under the weight of anxiety, remember the acronym PRESSURE for practical applications to relieve the strain of the constant panic you feel:

1. *Pop:* Pop your thought, that is. Picture imagery that really helped me was to think of my thoughts as bubbles. When I would start to play the "what if" line of thinking, increasing my rising panic, I would "pop" it in my mind in order to redirect my thoughts. It might be hard to do this if you are in true fight or flight, but practicing positive redirection of your thoughts on a day-to-day basis is extremely helpful in creating long-term habits for your mental wellbeing.

2. *Rest:* Don't stress about your stress. It has no impact on your ability to produce a child, so it's OK to feel what you need

to feel and embrace each emotion as it comes. Suppressing your feelings is counterproductive in your ability to be a healthy, functioning individual. Studies show anxiety and emotional duress experienced due to infertility do not negatively impact IVF rates.[3]

3. *Exercise:* Find a physical way to release those feelings. Mine was bike riding in the evenings! I would ride lap after lap in the coolness of the night around our neighborhood. That trusty old blue beach cruiser has seen a lot of tears.

4. *Share:* Find a safe outlet like a Christian counselor or trusted friend.

5. *Serve:* Find a way to use your story in a way that helps others. Feeling purpose from your pain is the *best* gift I can give you. "Anxiety weighs down the heart, but a kind word cheers it up." (Proverbs 12:25)

6. *Understand:* The first thing that sincerely helped me understand my anxiety was to identify my symptoms. "I know I am not dying right now. I know I am in the middle of a panic attack and it will eventually end. I just have to ride the wave." Also, becoming self-aware of your known triggers can give you an edge on beating them to the punch.

7. *Repeat:* Repeat things you know to be true: Bible verses and claiming God's Word are concrete things you can hold onto. "Can any one of you by worrying add a single hour to your life?" (Matthew 6:27) You can also repeat very basic facts like stating your name and address out loud.

8. *Equalize:* Equalize your hormones or brain chemicals. The core reason my anxiety got dangerously out of control was

due to my hormones dipping too low after coming off the fertility medication. I needed to adjust my progesterone and estrogen levels in order to get back to hormone neutral, which is still something I have to do to this day. If your anxiety feels out of control, don't wait to get help medically. A chemical imbalance isn't a matter of mental fortitude, and it doesn't make you weak for needing help.

Dear Lord,

I am overcome with anguish and uncertainty but your Word tells me not to be anxious about anything, but in every situation, by prayer and petition with thanksgiving, to present my requests to you. (Philippians 4:6) Help me to focus on your truths that are unchanging and give me the courage to use my pain for the good of others.

In Jesus' name, Amen.

Week One: *Pray healing over your body and that your womb would be opened.*

Day 3

GRIEVING

"The righteous cry out, and the Lord hears them; He delivers them
from all their troubles. The Lord is close to the brokenhearted
and saves those who are crushed in spirit. The righteous person
may have many troubles, but the Lord delivers him from them
all; He protects all his bones, not one of them will be broken."
Psalms 34:17-20

Grief is an inescapable force of nature that descends like a powerful
tsunami, wreaking havoc and obliterating everything in its path—
an all-consuming black cloud of sorrow that permeates every crack
and crevasse of your body and mind. Although your loss (the loss
of your child, for instance) is a singular event, the far-reaching
effects and new realities from which your grief emerges can be soul-
crushing. Elisabeth Elliot says, "Suffering and love are inextricably
bound up together. And love invariably means sacrifice."4 To love
is to suffer and to suffer is to love. To give an example, my friend's
mother had an affair and left their family suddenly when we were
in college. Although this was a singular event of abandonment,
loss, and trauma for my friend, the way in which new realities
emerged was equally as painful. Through the course of the divorce,
she uncovered life-altering details that affected her core identity.
Holidays at home looked drastically different and were now avoided,

learning to accept her mother's new husband and children, and so on. Like a catastrophic explosion, the residual shrapnel of perpetual loss that worked its way into her heart was also devastating. The unique lens through which you now view life and the newfound realities that emerge can be entirely overwhelming.

Our culture tends to view loss as something you leave in your past. How often have you heard the question, "Have you been able to move on?" asked to someone who has experienced loss? Can someone who has lost their legs fail to remember that they were once able-bodied? By no means. You cannot forget something that was once a part of you; instead, you learn how to adapt, survive, and hopefully thrive within your new set of limitations. The occurrence of tragedy similarly changes who we are down to our very DNA as we are forced to readjust to life within our own limitations of loss. Jerry Sittser said, "I did not go through pain and come out on the other side. Instead I lived in it and found within that pain the grace to survive and eventually grow."[5]

My husband and I often joke that the suffering we experienced has aged us in dog years. Like, take four years of infertility and sickness and grief and multiply by some number higher than five. We are definitely old souls. But though the growing and the stretching and the dying, we were introduced to our new selves and to new strength. Not that I would choose my suffering, mind you, but I cannot sit here and say I am not a more patient, caring, and empathetic individual because of it. Like a tree in the desert, my roots had to grow strong and deep to survive; consequently, I have confidence I will not be easily taxed in the storms ahead. I know that doesn't help you while carrying the weight of childlessness—as you sit on the sidelines with your face pressed to the glass, waiting for your chance at motherhood. If I told you in two more years you would most certainly, definitely, absolutely have a baby in your arms, you would be fine. Wouldn't you? It would resolve the tension of your aching desires with the unknown and the fear. I always said If I could just know that I would have a child one day, I could bear the infuriating in between—the paralyzing limbo. Like a pressure cooker set on maximum capacity, our grief writhes under the weight and intensity of a mother's love with no child to give it to. You didn't choose this cruel life. For some of us, that limbo will eventually resolve while others will continue to experience an enduring baby ache.

As helpless and paralyzing as this heavy veil of grief is that you bear, it is not the loss of your child, the mourning of motherhood, or the grief of childlessness that defines you. No, Sister. You are defined by things you have complete control over, namely your response to the hard parts of life. Our acceptance of this suffering and the humility to allow God to use it for whatever purposes He chooses can be the difference of continuing on in the land of the living or sitting life out in the sidelines of debilitating grief. Unfortunately, there is a due course to mourning your loss that has no shortcuts or detours. Here are a few things you can do to grow your roots stronger and deeper for survival in the desert:

1. *Unmask Your Grief:* Is your grief deceptively disguised by bitterness or anger? Your capability to get to the heart of your pain depends on your capacity to identify and peel back the ancillary layers grief projects. Unchecked anger can lead to bitterness and like a slow-growing cancer, smoldering bitterness within your heart can seep toxicity into every facet of life.

2. *Lean into the Pain:* As daunting as it sounds to dive head deep into the murky abyss of pain and suffering, the fastest way to true healing is through the eye of the storm. There can be a self-perceived pressure to resume normal life, continuing as the most present wife, mother, boss, etc., but

to genuinely find yourself again, you must allow yourself space to fully grieve.

3. *Find Balance in Your Suffering*: It's odd to say that there is an art to suffering, but it is indeed a delicate balance. You must allow yourself the awareness and submission to truly be present in your grief and to feel whatever it is that your emotions are dictating. On the flip side, permitting yourself to entirely succumb to the suffocating quicksand of sadness is not a space you want to stay in permanently either. "This is my comfort in my affliction, that your promise gives me life." (Psalms 119:50 ESV)

4. *Give Your Partner Grace:* We all suffer differently, so have patience and grace for your husband or your wife. One of my friends who just lost her child told me that her husband gave her the advice to set a date with grief at the same time every day to allow herself the space to mourn. If this isn't a perfect example of the waffles and the pancake analogy, I don't know what is! Men, generally speaking, have an easier time compartmentalizing their emotions. It highlights the beautiful differences of how we, as men and women, were created and how those differences permeate our grieving processes as well. Your projected grief might not look the same as your partners, so be willing to accept these differences.

5. *Express Yourself:* I would encourage you to put your pain to paper today. Painting, writing your story out, or simply putting down descriptor words on a piece of paper that expresses your feelings can be a practical way of processing the overwhelming emotions you feel.

Be merciful to me, Lord, for I am in distress; my eyes grow weak with sorrow, my soul and body with grief. My life is consumed with anguish and my years by groaning; my strength fails because of my affliction, and my bones grow weak. Let your face shine on your servant; save me in your unfailing love.

—Psalms 31:9-10, 16

Dear Lord,

I cry to you from the depths, for in my sorrow, I am weak. In you, I place my trust, O, Lord, and I repeat that day and night. Give me your peace that surpasses all understanding (Philippians 4:7) and have mercy on my soul.

In Jesus' name, Amen.

Week One: *Pray healing over your body and that your womb would be opened.*

Day 4

ADVERSITY

"In the day of prosperity be joyful, and in the day of adversity
consider: God has made the one as well as the other, so that
man may not find out anything that will be after him."
Ecclesiastes 7:14 ESV

"Adversity is the *prosperity* of the Great." No joke, this was in my
fortune cookie. Disclaimer: I don't think fortune cookies hold any
power past the paper they are printed on, but I cannot stop thinking
about the profound meaning nonetheless! Consider the Bible greats:
Noah, David, Lot, Daniel, and the list goes on. Rahab the prostitute,
Ruth the widowed foreigner, and Moses the exiled orphan all faced
tremendous affliction. Still, they are known because they pushed
through their trials, overcame their fears, endured their suffering,
and accomplished mighty things in the name of the Lord. None
were necessarily qualified for the task before them, but adversity
and the conscience choice to unwaveringly trust in God is the
common thread that made these individuals extraordinary. They
were empowered because of their adversity; moreover, you are who
you are because of your trials of infertility—not despite them.

But He said to me, "My grace is sufficient for you, for my power
is made perfect in weakness." Therefore I will boast all the more

gladly about my weaknesses, so that Christ's power may rest on me. That is why, for Christ's sake, I delight in weaknesses, in insults, in hardships, in persecutions, in difficulties. For when I am weak, then I am strong.

—2 Corinthians 12:9-10

Adversity lays bare our most authentic self, cutting through the ease of complacency and the shallowness of pure rhetoric to reveal several things. First, adversity reveals our genuine view of God. It's simple to say you trust a parachute while standing on solid ground watching skydivers glide down with ease, but when you are 15,000 ft. high and perilously hanging over the side of the plane is when push comes to shove. Do you trust it enough to jump out of the plane? If it gets twisted and isn't opening, do you trust the backup to save you before it's too late? Likewise, when you are in a complete life free fall, do you believe in God's sovereignty—His ultimate control over everything? Do you believe God is good, sincerely good, even if the parachute never opens?

It startled me in the midst of suffering when I suddenly didn't know if He was good and felt guilty for wrestling with the very idea of God. It is in this frantic free fall that we either allow our faith to stabilize us enough to pull the parachute or capitulate to the tailspin panic of absolute chaos. I can personally say that I know beyond a shadow of a doubt God is real, but let's say, for argument's sake, that there is no higher power—nothing beyond ourselves or this human experiment we've found ourselves in. Like a child in distress needing the comfort of his mother, my faith, at the very least, offers real hope and reassurance to combat the darkness this world radiates; for believing in nothing is the most terrifying thing of all.

Secondly, adversity reveals different things about ourselves such as: how we respond in high-stress situations, how we cope with anxiety, our attitude towards set circumstances, and uncovering newfound empathy. Adversity, moreover, reveals our actual capacity to endure. How many times have you said, "I can't imagine going through something like that!" and then find yourself smack dab in the middle of that very thing—the loss of a child, the loss of your job, or mourning something you have dreamed about since birth. You can endure much more and are considerably stronger than you anticipated. There is a self-assuredness and strength that alone comes through trial. Ecclesiastes 7:14 (quoted above) reveals that the Lord has determined no man be able to foresee his future, whether it be afflictive or prosperous so that we might live in constant dependence on God. I have found that in order to survive life's trials, we *must* believe in something other than ourselves. So today, when you feel overcome and overwhelmed because of your hardship, remember that no one of greatness experienced an easy, mediocre life. No Sister, they were forged in the fire and came out on the other side, not unscathed, but seasoned in grandeur.

> *No stars gleam so brightly as those which glisten in the polar sky, no water tastes so sweet as that which springs amid the desert sand, and no faith is so precious as that which lives and triumphs in adversity. Tried faith brings experience. You could not have believed your own weakness had you not been compelled to pass through the rivers; and you would never have known God's strength had you not been supported amid the water-floods. Faith increases in solidity, assurance, and intensity the more it is exercised with tribulation. Faith is precious, and its trial is precious too.*
>
> —*Strengthen my Spirit* by Charles Spurgeon[6]

Dear Lord,

Help me to fully embrace my adversity. Through these trials, I know that a great work is being produced within me. I will glory in my suffering because I know that suffering produces perseverance; perseverance, character; and character, hope. (Romans 5:3-4)

In Jesus' name, Amen.

Week One: *Pray healing over your body and that your womb would be opened.*

Day 5

SUFFERING

"Blessed is the man who remains steadfast under trial, for
when he has stood the test he will receive the crown of
life, which God has promised to those who love him."
James 1:12

As our pastor so often likes to say and I so often like to quote,
"We live in exile on planet death." It sounds considerably more
melodramatic coming from him with his theatrical South African
accent but in all seriousness, suffering is impartial to no one.
Christian, Jew, Muslim, Agnostic—we are all susceptible to the pain
this world has to offer. Just because I'm a "good Christian" leaves
me no more concealed to adversity than anyone else. Unfortunately,
the Bible even assures us we will experience hardship at some point
or another in our lives, but if you are reading this book then you
already know that to be true! Culture is quite persuasive with the
subtle indoctrination of happiness at all costs. Since the secular
presumption is that nothing exists beyond this life, it naturally lends
our present and perpetual happiness to be of paramount importance.
It's difficult in a comfort-driven society not to buy into the selfish
easiness of it all. Unfortunately, if happiness becomes your end goal
when suffering arises, it then compromises your very purpose for
existence. Subconsciously I had bought into the entitlement of a

pain-free life as a result of this wholehearted belief my devotion to God was cause for relief.

Suffering is a great motivator to know God deeply and experience Him profoundly, for it was here that I discovered who He really is. Without the prompting of pain, my awareness of His real character would have remained tragically shallow. C.S. Lewis said, "God whispers to us in our pleasures, speaks in our conscience, but shouts in our pain: it is His megaphone to rouse a deaf world."[7] While God allows suffering to occur, He is also actively involved in bringing redemption through it. We can be assured that our child dying or enduring a miscarriage was not a result of God's lack of love for us or His inability to save our child. Rather, through the Bible, we see God's love for us and our children here or in heaven, God's sovereign power to control life or death, and that through this power He is accomplishing His great and eternal purposes by way of our trials.

So how do we survive the cards we are dealt with and not give way to the resentful victimization that we feel; moreover, the injustice of it all? I played the "Why Me?" game for a long time, and it's an easy place to get stuck. It's truly not fair that others are happily and casually going on with their lives, and I am stuck in this limbo of never-ending agony. I think we have to take a step back and remember that our life here on earth is but a breath. Our hope is in Christ alone and not our own vacillating happiness. TobyMac, a Christian artist, tragically lost his 21-year-old son and his response was what we would all hope to claim in the midst of the greatest suffering imaginable: "My wife and I would want the world to know this: We don't follow God because we have some sort of under-the-table deal with Him, like, we'll follow you if you bless us. We follow God because we love Him. It's our honor. He is the God of the hills and the valleys. And He is beautiful above all things."[8]

The turning point for me was being able to accept my barrenness enough to shift my perspective and realize I had complete control over *how* I suffered. A fresh pair of glasses moved me from victim to vanquisher, and that small sense of control was empowering in a sea of helplessness. No one could take that from me—my response to the hard parts of life, what I did with the stripes that I bore, or how it affected others. Infertility or miscarriage may have written your first chapter. Regrettably, it might have stolen the second and third as well, but it doesn't take the ending! You command the final narrative so what will people say of you? What will be your legacy? I also realized my suffering was the very thing I could give back to the Lord as an offering of faithfulness. That portion was entirely within my control as well. We are never required to give more than we possess and I had nothing left but my crippled heart and a hollow womb. My barrenness was my five loaves of bread, my two small coins, and my jar of water. I was required to give the Lord whatever I had, but it was His job to feed the multitude, fill the church plate, and make wine flow. My faith amidst suffering was not the magical key that unlocked instant health, wealth, and happiness; it was the anchor to my ship, keeping it steady through the hurricane of hopelessness.

I pray for you today, Friend. I pray that in the depths of this suffering you bear, you would be immovable in your faith and present it before the Lord as your proclamation of faithfulness to Him. "Now to him who is able to do immeasurably more than all we ask or imagine, according to his power that is at work within us, to him be glory in the church and in Christ Jesus throughout all generations, for ever and ever! Amen." (Ephesians 3:20-21)

Dear Lord,

Allow my suffering to eradicate all preconceived notions of you in order that your true nature be revealed. Help me see your goodness despite the abandonment I feel. I strive for the humility to maintain a softened heart along with the courage to present my suffering as an offering of all that I have in this season of hardship. "Cast your cares on the Lord and He will sustain you; He will never let the righteous be shaken." (Palms 55:22)

In Jesus' name, Amen.

Week One: *Pray healing over your body and that your womb would be opened.*

Day 6

SPIRITUAL WISDOM

"… indeed, if you call out for insight and cry aloud for
understanding, and if you look for it as for silver and search for
it as for hidden treasure, then you will understand the fear of
the Lord and find the knowledge of God. For the Lord gives
wisdom; from his mouth come knowledge and understanding."
Proverbs 2:3-6

Wisdom cannot be taught, bought, and does not singularly come
with age, which means I have good news for you today: your door
prize for that hard-fought suffering you've endured is indeed wisdom.
You see, spiritual wisdom is grounded in our understanding of
how God works and our knowledge of his true character. Suffering
propels us to work out our faith in the nitty-gritty of life, seeking
His truth and understanding. As we grow more intimately with
God, develop a deep love and knowledge of His Word, and become
sensitive to the voice of the Holy Spirit, can we then gain insight
with His eternal perspective. Spiritual wisdom comes into play when
we disallow the bias of past hurts or present desires to cloud the
judgment of our decision-making or understanding of our current
circumstances. Wisdom of our own accord is polluted by sin and
subject to our own limitations, but wisdom from the Lord is first

pure, then peaceable, gentle, open to reason, full of mercy and good fruits, impartial and sincere. (James 3:17)

As I was trying to gain wisdom and understand my suffering through the lens of an eternal perspective, the line of questioning I kept coming back to was this:

1. Does God exist?
2. If He exists, then is He involved in our lives?
3. If He's involved in our lives, then does He have the power to change my circumstances?
4. If He has the power to change my circumstances and doesn't, is He good?
5. If God is good and cares about me personally and I continue to suffer, then what is the greater meaning of my present circumstances?

I thought I believed in God, but then life punched me in the face and left me wondering, Is He good? Is He actively participating in my story? And if He is, then that's concerning because my husband is potentially dying, I'm barren, and God is nowhere to be found. I was a ship without a sail being tossed violently in the sea of life's storms. But bit by bit, through the study of scripture and with the help of godly individuals possessing sound doctrine (like my pastor), I got to the other side of my faith—the one that's been tested and I know to be true. I've lived it!

I once had a woman at church tell me that I would get pregnant when God felt like I was ready and I deserved it. I was so taken back by her comment I was utterly speechless. I tried not to be offended but found myself increasingly sad for her since her theology lined up with my "performance-based God." *Once I confess that sin that somehow upset God, my blessings and life will get back on track and I will deserve good things again.* Spiritual wisdom, or rather someone's perception of God and its depth or shallowness really exposes their degree of suffering and their intensity to know God—to truly know Him intimately. The Bible tells us to search for wisdom like you would search for silver or gold, a priceless commodity in this game of life. To acquire true Godly wisdom is to be in possession of a rare treasure. So what "treasure" do you seek and how are you looking for it? This season of life can be exhausting, to say the least. Your perspectives shift, your priorities change, and the fragility of life is exposed. Don't let your preconceived notions of God impair your ability and desire to know Him fully. Spiritual wisdom, my Friend, is yours for the taking if you genuinely thirst for the knowledge of God.

Dear Lord,

Although I wouldn't choose my suffering, I know there is a great work being produced in me. James says if anyone lacks wisdom, ask for it. (James 1:5) So Lord, allow me to strengthen the foundation of my faith in order that I might understand your inner workings and see life through the lens of spiritual wisdom.

In Jesus' name, Amen.

Week One: *Pray healing over your body and that your womb would be opened.*

Day 7

ANGUISH + JOY

"Consider it pure joy, my brothers and sisters, whenever you face trials of many kinds, because you know that the testing of your faith produces perseverance. Let perseverance finish its work so that you may be mature and complete, not lacking anything."
James 1:2-4

Pregnancy after loss is never simple. It's guilt, paranoia, isolation, and anxiety. It's starting every sentence with "if" and not "when." It's holding your breath and waiting for the other shoe to drop. It's panicking when you feel kicks and it's panicking when they stop. It's anguish and joy mixed together with every other emotion in between. Anguish and joy find similarity in the intensity of emotion that they produce. Joy, as we see it in scripture, is always attached to something—such as the joy that's produced from the hope we have in Christ. Alternatively, anguish—as it is intended in scripture—is not only physical suffering but with the added element of mental distress attached to it. Anguish is my husband's missed heartbeats after his surgery with not only the component of physical suffering but with intense dread alongside that as a result of his trauma. Anguish is, also, our "Year of Death" when I not only had the hurt of infertility but also experienced heavy spiritual harassment (i.e., getting struck by lightning, debilitating panic attacks, etc.). Pain with anxiety, suffering with dread, and hurt with harassment all equal anguish. In 1 Samuel 1:1-16, we see Hannah in deep anguish over her infertility, so much so that the priest thought she was drunk. "Hannah replied, 'I am a woman who is deeply troubled. I have not been drinking wine or beer; I was pouring out my soul to the Lord. Do not take your servant for a wicked woman; I have been praying here out of my great anguish and grief." (v 15-16) Can you relate to the intensity of her weeping and pleading with the Lord?

Anguish and joy in their dividing magnitude can also coexist, as so beautifully exemplified in Motherhood. Is it not a space that creates the greatest of joys yet causes the deepest of sorrows, both mingling sometimes in the very same breath? In a beautiful twist of circumstances, the Lord will occasionally cause the source of our anguish to become the source of our joy. Personally speaking, the agony of my infertility battle has now become something I greatly value and the source of my joy in walking alongside other women traveling down the same path. God turned my pain into my passion. I'm the girl on the sidelines with the obnoxiously loud sign cheering you on at the hardest part of your race saying, "GO! Keep running! I not only see your pain, but I know it well and have confidence that you can make it! You are almost there, Sister!" Finally, in an active bringing about, your anguish is not meant to be indefinitely stagnant. Like the act of a woman in labor, it is intended to serve a short-term purpose in birthing something extraordinary.

Very truly I tell you, you will weep and mourn while the world rejoices. You will grieve, but your grief will turn to joy. A woman giving birth to a child has pain because her time has come; but when her baby is born she forgets the anguish because of her joy that a child is born into the world. So with you: Now is your time of grief, but I will see you again and you will rejoice, and no one will take away your joy. In that day you will no longer ask me anything. Very truly I tell you, my

Father will give you whatever you ask in my name. Until now you have not asked for anything in my name. Ask and you will receive, and your joy will be complete.

—John 16:20-24

The Lord is calling to you today. Will you bear down on your faith and trust God with your anguish? At the height of your tribulation He is actively bringing about the birth of a bigger story and something precious to you: the joy of a child, the joy of a ministry, the joy of friendships. The heaviness of the load that you bear may cause you to want to throw in the towel on God, but your pain is meant for more than the anguish you are currently experiencing, so *don't give up!* The darkest moments are before the coming dawn and Joy. Is. Rising.

Dear Lord,

Help me to endure my anguish because you have promised that my grief will turn to joy and I know your word does not turn void. (Isaiah 55:11) Allow me to see glimpses of hope, be comforted by your promises, and encouraged that this season of anguish is intended for more than just the pain I carry. It's meant to produce something miraculous!

In Jesus' name, Amen.

Week One: *Pray healing over your body and that your womb would be opened.*

WEEK 2
DAY 8-14

Day 8

SPIRITUAL OPPRESSION

"For our struggle is not against flesh and blood, but
against the rulers, against the authorities, against
the powers of this dark world and against the
spiritual forces of evil in the heavenly realms."
Ephesians 6:12

As Christians, we may rest assured that we can never be possessed by
the devil, but we certainly would be sorely remiss to underestimate
the supernatural war we are engaged in and the intense spiritual
oppression the devil wages this side of heaven. It might seem a
bit melodramatic to be taking cues from a scene right out of an
M. Night Shyamalan movie or comparing spiritual realms to the
alternate universe in The Matrix (*red pill or blue?*), but do not be
deceived! 1 Peter 5:8 says, "Be alert and of sober mind. Your enemy,
the devil, prowls around like a roaring lion looking for someone to
devour." While Jesus died on the cross, defeating death once for all,
He also permitted Satan dominion over this world until He returns
again. (Revelation 20:7) By discrediting or minimizing the devil's
power in your life and unwisely believing you are not susceptible
to his conniving schemes is akin to sauntering into battle naked,
making you the most vulnerable prey of all. A wise man once said,
"The greatest trick the devil ever pulled was convincing the world

he didn't exist."[9] If we believe, as Christians, that Jesus died and rose again but are ignorant to its very purpose in defeating the extremely real powers of Hell, then you cannot fully embrace the redemption of the cross! Therefore, if you accept and have faith in Jesus' miraculous resurrection, then you also must accept that there are indeed demonic forces present in our day-to-day life. "And having disarmed the powers and authorities, he made a public spectacle of them, triumphing over them by the cross." (Colossians 2:15)

The same Bible that talks of a legitimate God also talks of a legitimate devil who is ruthlessly scheming against your mind, body, and soul, searching for a stronghold or an area of weakness to harass, intimidate, and persecute. What is your area of weakness? Is it bitterness, envy, jealousy, discontentment, or low self-worth? The devil's ultimate goal is to get you so emotionally beat up that you are left too weak and overwhelmed to absorb God's truth, ultimately marring His immutable attributes and muddying His character. Like any good army commander, the devil is strategically and quietly attacking your most vulnerable weakness. It often starts with a hurt, wound, or disappointment and as a result our hearts become susceptible and fertile ground for Satan to plant his lies. For instance, let's say that in your inability to have a child, you start believing the lie that you have no value, no self-worth, and no purpose. Little by little, Satan builds his deceit, which consequently produces a distorted view of God and a skewed perception of yourself. Paul says, "For though we live in the world, we do not wage war as the world does. The weapons we fight with are not the weapons of the world. On the contrary, they have divine power to demolish strongholds." (2 Corinthians 10:3-4) An awareness of your insecurities, meditating on scripture while drawing near to God, and putting on the full armor of God (Ephesians 6) is the best defense we can utilize against his schemes. "Resist the devil and he will flee from you." (James 4:7 ESV)

I have personally found that as our suffering increased, so did the heavy cloud of spiritual oppression. The devil always attacks in periods of transition to thwart God's purposes and if he can ambush you at pivotal moments in your life then he can keep you from moving forward. Although God has given us the tools for claiming victory, the devil can absolutely limit the potential He has for us and cloud our judgment. According to Luke 4:2, Satan will tempt us to sin and prevent our efforts to obey God. Listen Sister, you cannot deplete God's power so stop allowing Satan to rob you of your joy and peace! As you are seemingly surrounded on all sides, the Lord is able to part the seas, turn water into wine, defeat any giant before you, and save you from the fire. Believe it to be true for your life!

Dear Lord,

"As for me, I call to God, and the Lord saves me. Evening, morning, and noon I cry out in distress, and He hears my voice. He rescues me unharmed from the battle waged against me, even though many oppose me." (Psalms 55:16-18) Allow my eyes to see the real war waged against me and give me victory, Lord!

In Jesus' name, Amen.

Week Two: *Pray for strength, resolve, and endurance in your suffering.*

Day 9
FEAR

"Have I not commanded you? Be strong and courageous.
Do not be afraid; do not be discouraged, for the Lord
your God will be with you wherever you go."
Joshua 1:9

Fear can be immobilizing, especially with infertility treatments where it can feel like you are taking fate into your own hands. I really struggled with paralyzation over a myriad of questions, namely:

Am I just not supposed to be a mom?

Do fertility treatments take control away from God?

*Does God know that something bad will happen if I
get pregnant, so that is why I cannot conceive?*

My everyday life was fraught with fears, both valid and irrational. My coping mechanism was to harden my heart to the longings that so desperately called to me from the deep. "I don't need a child," I would tell myself. When everyone and their mom would ask me when I was having children, I would so very casually recount my carefully crafted speech in which I selfishly wanted to be able to travel, advance my career, and spend more time with my husband Lane. *Way easier than telling the truth and the humiliation of obliterating my heart every time I was asked about kids.* When I realized, though, that I could not harden myself forever and the facade of indifference was still no barrier to the aching sadness I began to know sharply, I had to come face to face with my fears. Would I be able to move on if I never had children? *Probably not.* Would I regret it if I got to the end of my life and never exhausted all my options: IVF, adoption, etc.? *Yes!*

I could not let fear have its way: fear of what others thought, fear that just because it was not happening naturally meant God did not want me to have children, and fear of the unknown. Regarding IVF, I also concluded that if I had cancer, I would not ask God to heal me without also accessing modern medicine and getting treated with chemo or whatever procedures the doctor recommended within reason. Like David and his sling, although I was terrified, I had to step into battle and meet my giant halfway. After coming to this assertion and reaching my emotional breaking point, I stopped all infertility treatments and set a date for IVF: four months out. That definitive date gave me a great deal of peace amid the chaos. It allowed God time to move if He wanted to, but it also gave me a much-needed break and a hard next step.

Can I stop here just for a moment and speak to your heart, Sister? I know that infertility is not just about a negative pregnancy test. People have no clue about this journey from the outside looking in. Most think you are just sad because you're are not getting pregnant as fast as you had hoped; but infertility is painful and egregiously traumatic. It affects every aspect of your life—physical, mental, financial, and spiritual. Do not let the minimization of your heartbreak cause you to question yourself and get stuck. You are a true warrior. Our incredible doctor, *who as a Christian man had four children himself from IVF*, was used by God to help us through that precarious time and address our fears. Our sweet daughter Selah (*To Pause and Reflect*) James (*To Replace Sorrow with Joy*) is a gift from God, assisted by incredibly brilliant doctors and the technology we have available today. "I sought the Lord, and he answered me; he delivered me from all my fears." (Psalms 34:4)

So what are *your* fears? What's holding *you* up? I pray today you would look your fear right in the face and deny its power over your decision making. Is it the adoption papers you need to finish or the foster meeting you feel God calling you to? Is it being vulnerable with your story? Is it the fear of feeling like you will never leave this godforsaken valley of sorrow? Life boils down to things we can control and things we cannot and there are A LOT of things you cannot control when it comes to having children. So repeat after me: I am worthy of pursuing the things I desire! "For God gave us a spirit not of fear but of power, love, and self-control." (2 Timothy 1:7 ESV) Ask yourself if you are fully embracing the things you indeed have control over and blaze that trail!

Dear Lord,

It says in your word: do not fear, for you are with me; do not be dismayed for you are my God. You will strengthen me and help me; You will uphold me with your righteous right hand. (Isaiah 41:10) Give me grace in my fear, Lord, and a spirit of courage and boldness to overcome my uncertainty.

In Jesus' name, Amen.

Week Two: *Pray for strength, resolve, and endurance in your suffering.*

Day 10

HOPE

"For I know the plans I have for you," declares
the Lord, "plans to prosper you and not to harm
you, plans to give you hope and a future."
Jeremiah 29:11

How do we have defiant hope in the face of the storm, when the darkness enshrouds and the way seems too treacherous to bear? The opposite of hope is not hopelessness; it is fear—the fear of another miscarriage, the fear of never having children, the fear of finances in the face of an enormous IVF/IUI bill, the fear of simply making it through the day with a battered and aching heart, masking the anguish and the tears you feel bubbling up in every conversation. I hated it when friends or family would tell me, "Don't worry! You'll get pregnant," as if they had a crystal ball and knew something I did not. It infuriated me that they would offer hope they did not know for certain was possible and hope they had no right to give. Circumstances had robbed my innocence of a carefree outlook on life. I had to be realistic and I couldn't operate in the gray. The gray or that sliver of hope was too risky for my crippled heart to live in, so I am not going to sugar coat it for you either, Friend. I cannot promise you that there is a child at the end of your journey, that your body will be healed, or that you will get the "happily ever after" you have been dreaming of for so long. I know these are hard days and honestly, it might get worse before it gets better; but I can promise you there are ways to find confidence and purpose in this never-ending limbo of pain.

Getting out of bed might feel exhausting to you right now. Even reading through this list might seem overwhelming, but whatever you have to do to keep moving forward, do it—break it down, block out the extra, and focus on the next thing. Don't think about the next month or the next week or even the next day; focus on the next thirty minutes and the next task before you. For those of you who run, you know running is solely a game of mental fortitude. When the race gets hard and your mind tells you to stop, to quit, to walk is when you must block out the voice that's screaming everything hurts. You have to concentrate on one foot in front of the other and nothing else. Before you know it, you are a mile down the road and then two—the voice eases up, the road gets smoother, and your body settles in. So, here are a few things you can do to keep moving forward:

1. *Have Context:* Understand that we were not originally created to experience death or wrestle with grief. Loss was never meant to be apart of God's plan for our lives. For that reason, it is normal to feel unprepared for the hardship you are facing. No dress rehearsal would have ever sufficed to equip you. Loss will surprise us and devastate us every time.

2. *Give Thanks:* This might seem counterintuitive while suffering, but practicing gratitude in even the small things can allow us to feel contentment, which in turn produces joy. Not happiness mind you, but to delight in the treasures we do possess. Write out something you are thankful for once a day and try to be as specific as possible. Instead of saying things like, "I am thankful for my best friend," try using individual examples like, "I appreciated it when my best friend stopped by with my favorite cup of coffee. It

made me feel loved even though I'm hurting. I'm so grateful for people who care about me."

3. *Claim God's Word:* "I wait for the Lord, my soul waits, and in his word I hope;" —Psalms 130:5 ESV

   "Rejoice in hope, be patient in tribulation, be constant in prayer." —Romans 12:12

   "I waited patiently for the Lord to help me, and he turned to me and heard my cry." —Psalms 40:1 NLT

   "Hope deferred makes the heart sick, but a desire fulfilled is a tree of life." —Proverbs 13:12 ESV

4. *Find a New Hobby:* Focusing your energy on an activity you feel accomplished in and have a passion for can be both soothing for the soul and a much-needed reprieve: playing the piano, learning a foreign language, yoga, hiking, calligraphy, horseback riding, etc. Make sure you are carving out time for yourself.

5. *Get a Fur Baby:* As women, the need to nurture is engrained deep within our soul. A cat or a dog can help relieve some of the grief we feel and provide a sense of calm. I don't know what I would do without my dog, Louis!

6. *Have Grace for Unkind Comments:* Unfortunately, none of us will escape the barrage of comments about our childbearing: *"Why do you guys not have kids yet?" "When is number 2 going to make their debut?" "Once you stop trying, then you'll get pregnant." "At least…"*

Often, these comments do not come from a malicious place but rather from ignorance and probably just not knowing what to say. As cruel as these might feel, have enough grace to let them roll off your back.

7. *Set Positive Incentives:* Whether a trip, those shoes you have been eyeing, or a romantic dinner with your hubby at that new restaurant you have wanted to try, have fun things to look forward to! For every round of treatment we did, we had something fun set at the end of it in case things didn't work out. This helped me immensely.

Dear Lord,

Your word says that our hope in you is an anchor for the soul, firm and secure. (Hebrews 6:19) Allow your strength to permeate my day-to-day and help me to find hope that is everlasting. "I love you, O Lord, my strength. The Lord is my rock and my fortress and my deliverer, my God, my rock, in whom I take refuge, my shield, and the horn of my salvation, my stronghold. I call upon the Lord, who is worthy to be praised, and I am saved from my enemies. The cords of death encompassed me; the torrents of destruction assailed me; the cords of Sheol entangled me; the snares of death confronted me. In my distress I called upon the Lord; to my God I cried for help. From his temple he heard my voice, and my cry to him reached his ears." (Psalm 18:1-6 ESV)

In Jesus' name, Amen.

Week Two: *Pray for strength, resolve, and endurance in your suffering.*

Day 11

FELLOWSHIP

"Praise be to the God and Father of our Lord Jesus Christ,
the Father of compassion and the God of all comfort, who
comforts us in all our troubles, so that we can comfort those in
any trouble with the comfort we ourselves receive from God.
For just as we share abundantly in the sufferings of Christ, so
also our comfort abounds through Christ. If we are distressed,
it is for your comfort and salvation; if we are comforted, it is
for your comfort, which produces in you patient endurance of
the same sufferings we suffer. And our hope for you is firm,
because we know that just as you share in our sufferings,
so also you share in our comfort."
2 Corinthians 1:3-7

Friends that truly "get you" and allow you to be seen in your darkest
moments are paramount in enduring hardships. God did not create
us to be individual creatures; rather, we are hardwired to crave
connection with others. In the absence of that bond, suffering
abounds. There is no relationship so precious and so rich as one that
is traversed through trial and bonded in bereavement. Similarly, the
point at which our circumstances overtake us and our faith falters is
where true friendship and the sweetest of intimacy shines brightest;
but it is also here that many friendships disengage. The occurrence

of tragedy or loss sifts friendships in a way that only the sincerest survive. I have personally been guilty of stepping away from friends enduring great trials, telling myself, "Surely they will not want to recount their story again and again," or, "I'll call when they have had time to process." Whether it be a divorce or loss of a child or parent, it is certainly easier to avoid vulnerability than to engage in the constant heaviness they carry. It is biblical, though, that we walk alongside our brothers and sisters in Christ and shoulder the load they bear!

2 Corinthians 1:3-7 (quoted above) should give us courage that our "Father of compassion" will provide the comfort we need to shoulder each other's pain in order that we might give as we have been given to. Just as you have received an everlasting hope that grants you the strength to soldier on, as sisters in Christ, we should share in the "patient endurance" our suffering provides. I would encourage you twofold: have the vulnerability to let someone see your pain and the realization of your deepest fears and have the accountability to step into an exhausted friend's story to shoulder their grief, taking courage and humility of epic proportions. It is in these sacred moments of giving and accepting that our truest selves are revealed.

Are you so overwhelmed in your grief that you are terrified of opening your heart to others? Like a pebble being plucked from a dam, are you worried you will not be able to get it all stuffed back in and remain in control once the barrier has been broken? Or is it fear of judgment and failure that keeps you from sharing your struggles? I promise you, finding solace in the safety of friends who understand your hardship is life-giving! Let me be clear though; you need to make sure those to whom you entrust your story are trustworthy. I encourage you to find a support group or a single friend you can confide in this week. In this season of survival, do not deprive yourself of deep and authentic connections that can be a lifeline for enduring the storm.

Dear Lord,

"Turn to me and be gracious to me, for I am lonely and afflicted. Relieve the troubles of my heart and free me from my anguish. Look on my affliction and distress and take away my sins." (Psalms 25:16-18) I pray that you would allow me to find friends that would surround me in my grief and lift me up. Give me the strength and vulnerability to welcome the comfort my aching heart needs.

In Jesus' name, Amen.

Week Two: *Pray for strength, resolve, and endurance in your suffering.*

Day 12

FAITH

"Though he slay me, yet I will hope in him;"
Job 13:15

True faith is not automatic, is not linear, and is never complete. True faith is hard-fought, it is tested, it can be shaken, and it can be restored. It is not inherited, nor is it packed in your suitcase as you head to college. It is precious, cannot be contained by pre-set formulas, and requires true vulnerability. Faith is confidence in what we hope for and assurance about what we do not see. (Hebrews 11:1) Like any good contractor building a house in storm's way—fortifying the foundation and bolstering the frame—our faith similarly is built brick by brick, slowly and deliberately. I felt so much guilt and shame when my faith was decimated by life's storms. I knew God was there, but I felt angry and confused by His allowance of suffering and to what purpose it was serving in my life. The house I so surely thought was reliably sound was crumbling with the sifting of the sand. I quickly realized that building internal solidarity of my faith depended on the strength of its foundation and my "I do good things and God blesses me" doctrine was causing the roof to cave in. Hear me when I say this, God is not offended by our questions or by our doubt. In fact, He invites them! He doesn't just desire you once you have it all together. He wants our truest self—insecurities, uncertainty, and all. A parent doesn't love his child once the child loves him back. You would pursue your child to the ends of the earth. Wouldn't you? So God's love isn't dependent on our certainty of Him. That impregnable truth is the fortress of stability in a tornado of doubt.

Our faith journey also does not sway God one way or the other. "If I just increase my belief in God, *then* He will heal me." How often did I find my heart saying these words as if my lack of conceiving was stemming from an insufficient faith and trust in God. I do not presume to insinuate that God is not capable of healing or that He is not engaged in our good, but I do want to debunk the theory that your level of faith or intensity in piety, prayers, and devotion have a correlating value to God's willingness to heal you. I found myself subconsciously thinking that if I followed all of His commands and loved Him purely, then He would heal me; moreover, it was my lack of faith that was standing in the way of the child I so desperately wanted. When God calls us to have faith in Him, He's not looking for a checklist of good deeds or robotic zeal. He wants a heart of sincerity—a heart of love or anger and one of trust or doubt. So, give yourself grace when it comes to searching for God's truth and rebuilding or reinforcing your foundation of faith after circumstances have leveled it. Amidst life's darkest storms, we can joyfully and assuredly cling to the fearlessness our faith provides in being eternally anchored to our God, the ROCK of hope. "He alone is my rock and my salvation, my fortress; I shall not be greatly shaken." (Psalm 62:2 ESV)

So, where should our heart position be and what kind of faith should we strive for? I believe God desires a faith that is not dependent on our presumptions of Him, one that can deal with ambiguity, and a faith that reverberates loudly when He goes silent. I love the story of

Shadrach, Meshach, and Abednego. After refusing to bow down to their king's gods at the cost of their own lives, they displayed faith of unwavering assuredness.

> *Shadrach, Meshach and Abednego replied to him, "King Nebuchadnezzar, we do not need to defend ourselves before you in this matter. If we are thrown into the blazing furnace, the God we serve is able to deliver us from it, and he will deliver us from Your Majesty's hand. **BUT EVEN IF HE DOES NOT**, we want you to know, Your Majesty, that we will not serve your gods or worship the image of gold you have set up."*
> —Daniel 3:16-18

In the face of great trial, they simultaneously claimed victory yet surrendered completely to an unknown outcome. With every failed pregnancy test, or D&C, or insurmountable circumstance, our faith should proclaim, "But even if He does not!" It doesn't have to be a battle cry or a rebel yell. It can daily whisper, "Lord, I trust You." A brush of Jesus' garment heals and a mustard seed of faith moves mountains. So be encouraged that one foot in front of the other is all that you need in this season of life and nothing will be impossible for you. (Matthew 17:20) The God we serve is able to heal my body and give me a child, *but even if He does not*, yet I will hope in Him.

Dear Lord,

Give me the desire and the fortitude to daily trust in you. I pray my faith would be strengthened despite being challenged by things I cannot understand. "Though the fig tree does not bud and there are no grapes on the vines, though the olive crop fails and the fields produce no food, though there are no sheep in the pen and no cattle in the stalls, yet I will rejoice in the Lord, I will be joyful in God my

Savior. The Sovereign Lord is my strength; he makes my feet like the feet of a deer, he enables me to tread on the heights." (Habakkuk 3:17-19)

In Jesus' name, Amen.

Week Two: *Pray for strength, resolve, and endurance in your suffering.*

Day 13

DESIRES

"Take delight in the Lord, and He will give
you the desires of your heart."
Psalms 37:4

One of the most frustrating things to grapple with is reconciling our desires to our circumstances when they are not matching up. Like trying to fit a round peg of desire into the square hole of life, the injustice of an empty womb or an empty crib can drive you to the brink of all-consuming insanity. Confusion and heartbreak co-mingle into a feeling of rejection, knowing that the same God who has instilled the desire for children, the strong urge to nurture, and the ability to provide love wholeheartedly is the same one who is seemingly answering your prayers for now with a hard "No." It was simultaneously reassuring, knowing that the God who created my innermost being and knit me in my mother's womb was surely trustworthy in being faithful to take care of my deepest needs. I kept telling God, "If I am not able to have a child, then take away the desire to have one! Give me the longing for other things. If you don't heal me, then just give me the strength to endure another day."

As hard as it is to weather the waiting, there are several precious things born out of delayed desire. It is important to note that,

"Hardships often prepare ordinary people for an extraordinary destiny."10, 11 Therefore, I believe that God draws on our desperation to push us into our designated purpose. Just as winning the war on weight loss or debt requires a certain level of disgust of our current circumstances, desperation breaks through barriers otherwise not penetrable. Providing the endurance and motivation needed to weather the course, desperation fuels the "why" in any situation. For instance, my motivation to help others experiencing infertility is propelled by the depth of pain I know you're experiencing. "Why" do I want to help others? Because I never want anyone to feel as isolated as I did. Secondly, experience is the birthplace of empathy. Genuine empathy is solely learned through the hard-knock school of experience, and its teacher is suffering. To exist in the emotional complexity of a situation is to truly understand the totality of its ramifications. It is in this awareness that connection with others on a deeper and more profound level can be established. During my infertility journey, there was a bonding reassurance from friends who knew the same suffering I was going through. I could relax in their presence and not put on a pretense or cringe at the well-meaning comfort they offered. This is why I want to be open with my journey—to let you know I understand your tears, your screams into your pillow, and your exhausted desperation. You are *not* alone.

Do you truly trust that the Lord sees your needs, your desires—the ones so deep down they make your bones ache? Do we have faith that the Lord will be tender and gracious and honoring of those desires? I'm challenging myself with this one today too, Friend. Let us hold out, with open hands, our deepest and rawest longings, as meaningful or menial as they might seem, and trust that the God of all creation knows our hearts, our devotion to Him, and is working in our favor. "Let us hold unswervingly to the hope we profess, for he who promised is faithful." (Hebrews 10:23)

Dear Lord,

You know my heart and you see my tears. You understand my deepest desires because you created them and put them there. "You have searched me, Lord, and you know me. You know when I sit and when I rise; you perceive my thoughts from afar. You discern my going out and my laying down; you are familiar with all my ways. Before a word is on my tongue you, Lord, know it completely. You hem me in behind and before, and you lay your hand upon me." (Psalms 139:1-5) Be gentle with me Lord and allow me to feel your presence.

In Jesus' name, Amen.

Week Two: *Pray for strength, resolve, and endurance in your suffering.*

Day 14

THE WILL OF GOD

"Then David said to the Philistine [Goliath], 'You come to me with a sword and with a spear and with a javelin, but I come to you in the name of the Lord of hosts, the God of the armies of Israel, whom you have defied. This day the Lord will deliver you into my hand, and I will strike you down and cut off your head. And I will give the dead bodies of the host of the Philistines this day to the birds of the air and to the wild beasts of the earth, that all the earth may know that there is a God in Israel, and that all this assembly may know that the Lord saves not with sword and spear. For the battle is the Lord 's, and he will give you into our hand.'"
1 Samuel 17:45-47 ESV

How do we ascertain the will of God? Receiving concrete clarity is not a luxury we are always afforded, especially in times of great suffering and trial. There are several aspects to God's will that we must first consider in order for us to fully understand its impact on our decision making. First is God's providential will, which was set in stone from the beginning of time and cannot be changed. This is God's purpose in redeeming creation, defeating death, and receiving glorification for all time. Second is God's personal will for our lives, impacting our day-to-day decisions. We need to stop thinking that just because something is easy, or feels good, or falls into place that this alone is validation for the will of God in our lives. Most times, discovering His will means walking towards an unsure outcome. This, in turn, creates a faith where your heart is confident of what your mind does not yet know. David spoke victory over Goliath before the battle had even begun, yet he had to initiate a courageous plan of action and step into faith under very uncertain circumstances. In fact, his circumstantial probability of beating Goliath looked grim at best.

To set the stage: David was a young boy tending his father's sheep when he was instructed to bring food to his older brothers in battle and return with word of their well-being. When all of Saul's battle-hardened army remained terrified in challenging Goliath, David, a young boy too small to even wear the appropriate armor, answered the call. He stepped forward in confidence and simultaneously into God's faithfulness in giving him victory. As you are trying to discover God's personal will for your life, here are some simple guidelines to utilize in your decision making:

1. *Prayer and Surrender:* Ask the Lord specifically to shed light on your question of direction. I promise you if you seek God fervently and intentionally, He will be gracious in answering you. It might not be immediate and it might not be the answer you expected, but He will show up. If God is remaining silent for now, allow your heart to be bold enough to step into the plan you have formulated.

2. *Obey His Word:* Has God already revealed the answers you seek through His Word? He has clearly lined out truths in the Bible for us to follow; therefore, God's moral will is absolute. For instance, He is not going to bless your efforts in deceiving your spouse, nor would it ever be in His will for you to do so.

3. *Listen to Your Intuition:* The Holy Spirit has a keen way of guiding our conscience. Be still and listen to His leading but be careful not to mistake fear for the Spirit telling you not to move forward. Daniel would never have gone into battle with a sling and a stone if he had given way to fear. God has also given us the ability for discernment, so ask Him for wisdom.

   Alternatively, like Jonah, do you know exactly what the Lord is calling you to but fear stepping into the plan He has laid out for you? "The word of the Lord came to Jonah son of Amittai: 'Go to the great city of Nineveh and preach against it, because its wickedness has come up before me.' But Jonah ran away from the Lord and headed for Tarshish." (Jonah 1:1-3) Don't be swallowed by a whale in your quest for safety!

4. *Seek Godly Counsel:* The Lord has used sermons from our pastor, input from fellow believers (including my wise husband), and advice from my Christian counselor to affirm decisions or push me towards action. Be wise in granting the right people influence over your life. "Where there is no guidance, a people falls, but in an abundance of counselors there is safety." (Proverbs 11:14 ESV)

In reference to our discussion on God's sovereignty and the correlating significance of free will: if you can rule out that the direction you are headed does not violate God's concrete moral will for your life, then He has truly given you complete authority and freedom to make decisions. I don't believe God is playing some secret game of twister that constitutes His will for our lives. Like if we are oblivious in putting our left foot on red while pretzeled underneath our right hand on yellow, He's going to be utterly disappointed. Moving on faith is most often moving into fear and action is required for God to reveal Himself. David could have been defeated and maybe you will experience failure, but if you don't show up for battle and engage in the highs and lows of life you will never be able to fully realize the fullness God has for you. What if you miss out on the beauty of God's redemption and faithfulness? Don't let fear inhibit you for fear can cause you to get stuck in a place void of favor or failure. "For God gave us a spirit not of fear but of power and love and self-control." (2 Timothy 1:7 ESV)

Maybe the thing you feel God calling you to is just a stepping-stone to birth the thing you were really meant to do. When I felt God calling me to begin Hope Infertility Support Group, I knew undeniably the Holy Spirit was pressing on my heart in such a profound way. I *had* to answer the call. I was not a certified counselor, did not feel qualified in my volatile emotional state of being, and had no clue what I was doing—I just knew there were no Christian support groups in the area and I had to throw a lifeline of assistance to other women in need. I met with my church to get support, printed out at least 100 business cards, and dropped them off at multiple fertility clinics in Orlando. For the first six months, one girl showed up; just one. The following three months after that, no one showed up. I kept thinking that maybe God just wanted to ascertain my own willingness to answer the call. Maybe it was not about the group at all but more the submissiveness and obedience of my own grieving heart. Since 2015, our online group has slowly grown and I have been able to love on and encourage women one-on-one when they find me through our church advertisement. A precious ministry that, though small, has hopefully had an eternal impact.

God uses the most unqualified among us to make His name known. Are you stuck between a rock and a hard place of fear and indecisiveness? Do not allow the devil to rob you of victory over the Goliaths in your life and walk assuredly into God's will.

Dear Lord,

"O God, you are my God; earnestly I seek you; my soul thirsts for you; my flesh faints for you, as in a dry and weary land where there is no water. Because your steadfast love is better than life, my lips will praise you." (Psalm 63:1, 3) Give me peace and assurance to show up for battle and to embrace uncertainty, knowing your faithfulness is forthcoming and victory is imminent. "Let the words of my mouth and the mediation of my heart be acceptable in your sight, O Lord, my rock and my redeemer." (Psalm 19:14 ESV)

In Jesus' name, Amen.

Week Two: *Pray for strength, resolve, and endurance in your suffering.*

WEEK 3
DAY 15-21

Day 15

ENDURANCE

"I have fought the good fight, I have finished
the race, I have kept the faith."
2 Timothy 4:7 ESV

Can you imagine if you had all the money in the world and no problems? Sounds great, right? I would propose, though, the initial flame of self-indulgence would soon taper into a smoldering emptiness. If life never presented any challenges you would live in mediocrity at best, removing your need for God. Some of my most precious and treasured moments have been in overcoming seemingly insurmountable adversity. Great men and women who have left their mark on history were almost always born of adversity. Extraordinary people are known not necessarily for their circumstances but by their ability to rise above their current sufferings. Look at Theodore Roosevelt, who was paralyzed from the waist down by polio when he was 39, well before running for office and becoming President of the United States. Albert Einstein couldn't speak until he was three years old and was unemployed several years after college but went on to develop the theory of relativity. Born into poverty, Oprah Winfrey was abused during her adolescent years and lost a child in infancy that she delivered at only 14 years old. She proceeded on to score the highest-rated TV show in history and has been ranked the greatest black philanthropist in American history. Joni Eareckson Tada, a quadriplegic at 18 because of a diving accident, went on to be an advocate and speaker for the disabled and has written over 40 inspirational books.

You are made known because you endure—the greater the endurance, the more profound the legacy. You see, your capacity to endure solidifies your strength of character and your strength of character establishes your ability to overcome. Let us turn the tables on your grief for a minute. Consider you have been given a gift—not the cancer itself or the divorce proceedings or the empty womb, but the ability to rise above and to make your name known. I'm not trying to go all holier-than-thou martyr on you, but truly our attitudes can drastically alter the course for which we tread. The common thread with the individuals listed above was their attitude toward life after significant hardship. Not that they didn't have their moments of darkness and self-doubt because I am sure they did, but ultimately, they believed life was worth living and living to its fullest. They concluded they were worthy of success and had hope for good things to come.

Has infertility broken you? Has it taken your innocent dreams of motherhood and shattered them into a million horrific pieces? Bearing hardship is not easy. The art of enduring is sustaining increased mental fortitude while simultaneously engaging in hopeful vulnerability—a harmonious toughening and softening of the heart. Without the mental fortitude, you would be crushed under the weight of suffering and without the hopeful vulnerability, your heart will become bitter and withdrawn. I became so weary and emotionally tapped in the valley of infertility that I could not even attend church anymore. I reached my tipping point one Sunday when the pastor gave the altar call and I had to run to the car for relief before bursting into tears because the heaviness was too much to bear. It was like the raw nerve that I was hyper-aware of kept getting picked at and flayed open repeatedly. I had to take a break, not from God necessarily as I feel like I was still constantly crying out to him, but from things that would aggravate the already consuming misery assaulting me. I had to turn off worship music for a while, start saying no to baby showers, and pull away from certain friendships.

It's OK to say "No" to make it, but just be wary of withdrawing so much that you get lost in the black hole of isolation and self-pity. There is a fine balance to engaging in life and yet retreating enough to maintain your preservation level through the storm. Time will eventually fade your wounds and it will not always be this hard. Those in remission have a new lease on life and my arduous journey into motherhood has given me a depth of daily gratefulness otherwise forgotten. I know it is easier for me to objectively pontificate on the other side of infertility, to see it in its entirety and not be overcome by the potential variables. I can run my hands over the redeemed scar of barrenness and feel the weight of its totality rather than cower in fear from an unpredictable looming verdict. But it is where *you* are that the battle is won. The steeper the climb the more breathtaking the view and I believe your story is poised for a great victory.

Write these verses out and meditate on them today:

Hebrews 10:36
James 1:4
Colossians 1:11-12
James 1:12

Dear Lord,

I am so weary from the load I bear, but I know I can do all things because you strengthen me. (Philippians 4:13) I pray not only for strength in enduring but that my testament to suffering would be a light to others. I know your grace is sufficient for me, for your power is made perfect in my weakness. Therefore, I will boast all the more gladly of my weaknesses, so that the power of Christ may rest upon me. (2 Corinthians 12:9)

In Jesus' name, Amen.

Week Three: *Pray for your future Child/Children.*

Day 16

COURAGE

"Then the king commanded, and Daniel was brought and cast into the den of lions. The king declared to Daniel, 'May your God, whom you serve continually, deliver you!' And a stone was brought and laid on the mouth of the den, and the king sealed it with his own signet and with the signet of his lords, that nothing might be changed concerning Daniel. Then the king went to his palace and spent the night fasting; no diversions were brought to him, and sleep fled from him."
Daniel 6:16-18 ESV

Most Christians have heard the story of Daniel in the lion's den, but have you ever actually placed yourself in his shoes and tried to envision what he must have been feeling as they were rolling the stone shut? The slowly enveloping darkness quickly consuming the light with a suffocating terror. What were his thoughts in the blinding darkness as he shuffled around the damp mustiness of the cave? I am sure he felt abandoned at the malicious and unjust sentence forcing him to face the deadly growls inching closer and closer. Have you lived this very scene as the doctor walked in and said, "It's cancer," or, "I am sorry but there is no heartbeat"? It is an existential moment so horrifying you seem to watch your body from a blurry distance. Have you ever had the thought, "Is this *really* how it ends? Is this actually *my* story?" I have. I've looked into the eyes of my husband and not known if he was going to make it. I have sat late at night on the empty floor of my would-be nursery and desperately cried to the Lord for a child. David said in Psalms, "Be strong, and let your heart take courage, all you who wait for the Lord." (Psalms 31:24 ESV)

Sorely misguided comfort I often received from fellow believers was: "God will never give you more than you can handle." While 1 Corinthians 10:13 promises us that the devil will not be able to tempt us beyond our ability, nowhere does scripture suggest that God in any way limits suffering based on our ability to withstand it. Divorce destroys families, cancer ravages bodies, war devastates nations, and death eventually comes to all. Loss pulls back the curtain on the illusion of control and forces us to quickly realize our own limitations. I didn't feel like I was within a safe comfort zone of suffering, rather I felt absolutely overtaken and overcome with fear. I was in the lion's den. In my darkest moments, courage did not come from the hope of being healed for God has not guaranteed healing this side of heaven. Physical restoration was something I longed for but could not solidly cling to. The lifeline of courage I held on to for dear life was the concrete promise that my free gift of salvation was secure and eternal life with God was the larger end goal to my current short-term suffering. "According to his great mercy, he has caused us to be born again to a living hope through the resurrection of Jesus Christ from the dead, to an inheritance that is *imperishable, undefiled, and unfading*, kept in heaven for you." (1 Peter 1:3-4)

We all die and the ramifications of loss will affect us all sooner or later. That conclusion should not come as a surprise, but the reality of our fragility can allude us when life is good. Vacations, financial success, beautiful homes, and peaceful neighborhoods can all dull the reality that our lives could soon be gone. "All flesh is like grass and all its glory like the flower of grass. The grass withers, and the flower falls, but the word of the Lord remains forever." (1 Peter 1:24-25 ESV) Without the hope of Christ, decimating loss can become a place from which we do not emerge. Our courage as Christians should come from knowing that healed or not, the Lord has promised us an eternal inheritance in Heaven with Him. The courage to fight and to make this life worth living amid great loss comes from knowing the end score.

Daniel's courage prevailed and the Lord was gracious to save him from imminent death. Let your heart be brave today, knowing your current sufferings have a purpose in pointing to the glorification of God here and in heaven. Write out the following verse on an index card and insert your name in replace of Daniel's. Repeat this to yourself when you need a dose of courage!

> *I make a decree, that in all my royal dominion people are to tremble and fear before the God of* ***[Your Name Here]***, *for he is the living God, enduring forever; his kingdom shall never be destroyed, and his dominion shall be to the end. He delivers and rescues; he works signs and wonders in heaven and on earth, he who has saved* ***[Your Name Here]*** *from the power of the lions.*
> —Daniel 6:26-27 ESV

Dear Lord,

Thank you for your gift of eternal life and for giving me a solid foundation upon which to stand when there is nothing else to cling to. The courage to withstand the storm rests solely on the knowledge that you have already won the battle and my hope in you is secure. "Though I walk in the midst of trouble, you preserve my life; you stretch out your hand against the wrath of my enemies, and your right hand delivers me. The Lord will fulfill his purpose for me; your steadfast love, O Lord, endures forever. Do not forsake the works of your hands." (Psalms 138:7-8 ESV)

In Jesus' name, Amen.

Week Three: *Pray for your future Child/Children.*

Day 17

CRAZY TOWN

"And Sarai said to Abram, 'Behold now, the Lord has prevented me from bearing children. Go in to my servant; it may be that I shall obtain children by her.' And Abram listened to the voice of Sarai. So, after Abram had lived ten years in the land of Canaan, Sarai, Abram's wife, took Hagar the Egyptian, her servant, and gave her to Abram her husband as a wife. And he went in to Hagar, and she conceived. And when she saw that she had conceived, she looked with contempt on her mistress. And Sarai said to Abram, 'May the wrong done to me be on you! I gave my servant to your embrace, and when she saw that she had conceived, she looked on me with contempt. May the Lord judge between you and me!' But Abram said to Sarai, 'Behold, your servant is in your power; do to her as you please.' Then Sarai dealt harshly with her, and she fled from her."
Genesis 16:2-6 ESV

You are *not* crazy! OK, well maybe a little crazy. But what you are going through is so incredibly hard and your emotional response to those things is so incredibly normal. That's what I would have told my infertile self if I could wave a magic wand and go back in time. I would have sat her down and said, "Even though you feel like you are teetering on the emotional brink, so does every other stinking female walking this road." And when I say infertility, I am referring to the collective family of infertility: secondary infertility, miscarriage, etc. Crazy is normal on this roller-coaster ride. The first thing we must realize about our journey to bearing children is that to love is to suffer as we spoke about previously. It's really the first lesson of motherhood. The odd thing, for me, about not being able to conceive was that every day I mourned the loss of a child not even realized. I grieved the absence of motherhood so viscerally, even though I had not lost anything tangible. It is hard to validate the level at which you are suffering when there is nothing to quantify, but there is no set equation for how you should feel. And there is no "appropriate" level of crazy on your quest for kids.

Now, if I can validate your madness for a moment, let's take a look at Sarai [Sarah] in Genesis. Nothing like another woman conceiving your 86-year-old husband's baby after decades of trying to really push your infertile crazy over the edge. Am I right? Abram [Abraham], Sarah's husband, was one of the forefathers of our faith. The Lord made a covenant with him through which the savior of the world would come.

> *And he [God] brought him outside and said, "Look toward heaven, and number the stars, if you are able to number them." Then he said to him, "So shall your offspring be." And he believed the Lord, and he counted it to him as righteousness."*
> —Genesis 15:5-6 ESV

Most likely, the things going through Sarah's mind when she thrust her handmaiden on her amenable husband was an overwhelming sense of frustration, impatience, anxiety, and desperation even though the Lord had promised her and Abraham a child. Somewhere in her seventies, her ever-so-dead biological clock groaned with every palpable heartbeat. Tick-Tock, Tick-Tock, Tick-Tock. The unfortunate thing about her hasty plan was that she probably didn't think much past the part where Hagar actually conceives a child. In the very instant Hagar announced she was pregnant, the crushing shame of all those years of barrenness fell solely at Sarah's feet and she knew she was to blame for their infertility woes. It's one thing when your friend tells you she's pregnant after you've been trying for some time, but certainly quite another if your friend told you she was pregnant with your husband's child after years of heartbreak—the tipping point of crazy. Her shame and jealousy and bitterness drove her to physically harm Hagar in a flash of rage but thankfully the story doesn't end there. I'll give you a sneak peek of the ending. The Lord followed through on his promise to Sarah and she conceived her son Isaac at ninety years old.

> *Abraham was a hundred years old when his son Isaac was born to him. And Sarah said, "God has made laughter for me; everyone who hears will laugh over me."*
>
> —Genesis 21:5-6 ESV

Hear me, Sister, when I say that God's delays are not necessarily his denials. What drives us to the brink might be our tipping point of crazy but not the end of our story. The Lord was faithful to Sarah and He will be faithful to you as well. Maybe not a naturally conceived baby at the age of ninety, but I'm sure we can all agree that outcome wouldn't be our first option! As you question your sanity with the complexity of hormones and drugs and mental health, others minimizing your pain and trauma, worry, and on and on, remind yourself that the craziness you feel is completely normal. I'm sure every woman going through infertility can attest to this very thing.

Dear Lord,

As I struggle to find emotional stability amidst the turbulent waters of infertility, allow your power to be made perfect in my weakness.

"But he said to me, 'My grace is sufficient for you, for my power is made perfect in weakness.' Therefore I will boast all the more gladly of my weaknesses, so that the power of Christ may rest upon me." (2 Corinthians 12:9 ESV) Give me the strength to cling solidly to the hope of your faithfulness. I pray you would be preparing my heart to receive the long-awaited child I continue to hope for.

In Jesus' name, Amen.

Week Three: *Pray for your future Child/Children.*

Day 18

PRAYER

"After they had eaten and drunk in Shiloh, Hannah rose. Now Eli the priest was sitting on the seat beside the doorpost of the temple of the Lord. She was deeply distressed and prayed to the Lord and wept bitterly. And she vowed a vow and said, 'O Lord of hosts, if you will indeed look on the affliction of your servant and remember me and not forget your servant, but will give to your servant a son, then I will give him to the Lord all the days of his life, and no razor shall touch his head.' As she continued praying before the Lord, Eli observed her mouth. Hannah was speaking in her heart; only her lips moved, and her voice was not heard. Therefore Eli took her to be a drunken woman. And Eli said to her, 'How long will you go on being drunk? Put your wine away from you.' But Hannah answered, 'No, my lord, I am a woman troubled in spirit. I have drunk neither wine nor strong drink, but I have been pouring out my soul before the Lord. Do not regard your servant as a worthless woman, for all along I have been speaking out of my great anxiety and vexation.' Then Eli answered, 'Go in peace, and the God of Israel grant your petition that you have made to him.' And she said, 'Let your servant find favor in your eyes.' Then the woman went her way and ate, and her face was no longer sad."

1 Samuel 1:9-18 ESV

There is an undeniable mystery in the power and effectiveness of prayer. Our capacity to fully understand the ways of God are obviously limited by our own finite minds, bound by the constraints of time and divine knowledge. This mystery of prayer, therefore, is not necessarily something we can know everything about, but it is not something we can know nothing about either. One question within the mystery of prayer that plagued me while my husband and I were suffering was, "Does prayer change the will or mind of God?" And at the heart of that question was, "Will fervent prayer for a child cause God to potentially intercede on my behalf and be merciful in giving me one?" In other words, do we have influence over God regarding the circumstances in our life or is His will already set and unchangeable? As I was searching for this answer, I read many commentaries that proposed we do not have any influence over the concrete will of God. It suggested since God's nature is unchangeable and immutable, it would be a contradiction of His character for Him to "change his mind," so to speak. "For I the Lord do not change;" (Malachi 3:6) I also personally experienced times where it seemed like prayer after prayer fell on deaf ears and into empty space, egging on this notion that maybe God is indeed immovable.

In the midst of the greatest suffering I've endured, I have either known the sweetest, most intimate of divine connections or the eerie silence of hollow prayers and nothing in between. The proximity of God in the context of suffering feels either purposefully present or unnervingly absent. And the "unnervingly absent" reality was not only extremely disheartening but also demotivating for a thriving prayer life. As selfish as it sounds, if my prayers had no impact on the prospect of motherhood, then why even waste the little emotional energy I retained? Can you relate to these same feelings? All this to say, after many thought-provoking conversations with spiritual mentors and a thorough study of scripture, I would submit a resounding *YES*. Yes, God does hear our prayers, can intercede on our behalf, grant mercy, and cause change without challenging His overall providential will. Let me assert my claim by walking you through several pieces of scripture that were profound in my quest for understanding.

"And he told them a parable to the effect that they ought always to pray and not lose heart." —Luke 18:1 ESV

The Lord desires for us to pray!

"… then let those who are in Judea flee to the mountains. Let the one who is on the housetop not go down to take what is in his house, and let the one who is in the field not turn back to take his cloak. And alas for women who are pregnant and for those who are nursing infants in those days! **Pray that your flight may not be in winter or on a Sabbath.** For then there will be great tribulation, such as has not been from the beginning of the world until now, no, and never will be." —Matthew 24:16-21 ESV

> *This scripture is an interesting one. Jesus is speaking directly to the disciples about hardships preceding the tribulation and by the line "pray that your flight would not be in winter or on a Sabbath" (max traveling distance would of been 2,000 cubits outside the city walls) seems to suggest wiggle room for God to enact change and grant mercy without altering the overall greater plan of his return.*

"Then Abraham drew near and said, "Will you indeed sweep away the righteous with the wicked? Suppose there are fifty righteous within the city. Will you then sweep away the place and not spare it for the fifty righteous who are in it? Far be it from you to do such a thing, to put the righteous to death with the wicked, so that the righteous fare as the wicked! Far be that from you! Shall not the Judge of all the earth do what is just?" And the Lord said, "If I find at Sodom fifty righteous in the city, I will spare the whole place for their sake." Abraham answered and said, "Behold, I have undertaken to speak to the Lord, I who am but dust and ashes. Suppose five of the fifty righteous are lacking. Will you destroy the whole city for lack of five?" And he said, "I will not destroy it if I find forty-five there." Again he spoke to him and said, "Suppose forty are found there." He answered, "For the sake of forty I will not do it." Then he said, "Oh let not the Lord be angry, and I will speak. Suppose thirty are found there." He answered, "I will not do it, if I find thirty there." He said, "Behold, I have undertaken to speak to the Lord. Suppose twenty are found there." He answered, "For the sake of twenty I will not destroy it." Then he said, "Oh let not the Lord be angry, and I will speak again but this once. Suppose ten are found there." He answered, "For the sake of ten I will not destroy it." And the Lord went his way, when he had finished speaking to Abraham, and Abraham returned to his place." Genesis 18:23-33 ESV

Although God foreknew only a few righteous people remained (Lot and his family) in the City of Sodom and Gomorrah, we still see God graciously negotiating with Abraham and allowing him to intercede on behalf of the city.

"Again I say to you, if two of you agree on earth about anything they ask, it will be done for them by my Father in heaven. For where two or three are gathered in my name, there am I among them." — Matthew 18:19-20 ESV

"Then God remembered Rachel, and **God listened to her and opened her womb.** She conceived and bore a son and said, "God has taken away my reproach." And she called his name Joseph, saying, "May the Lord add to me another son!" —Genesis 30:22-24 ESV

What we see throughout scripture is not a contradiction of God's character but rather a paradoxical mystery within the power of prayer. What I concluded was that the God of all creation, who is both omniscient and unchanging, also invites our prayers and suggests a willingness to move on our behalf. It seems though, what influence we do have within God's individual will for our lives is entirely dependent upon a certain heart position. The requirements we see exemplified by the stories of Hannah and others are a healthy fear of God, reverence, respect, humility, faith, and sincerity. One requirement we do not see is our level of goodness or our closeness to God having a correlating advantage to our prayers. King Ahab, by far one of the most wicked kings in the Old Testament, ultimately sought forgiveness and prostrated himself before the Lord. The Lord was, therefore, gracious in hearing his request and thus spared his life.

> *Have you seen how Ahab has humbled himself before me? Because he has humbled himself before me, I will not bring the disaster in his days;*
>
> —1 Kings 21:29 ESV

Finally, I can attest firsthand that the Lord absolutely responds when you seek Him fervently in prayer. After fasting and praying with my husband for 21 days like my life depended on it (*because it did*), God spoke to me directly three long months later and gave me hope that a child was coming. Now, I'm not saying that just because you pray the Lord will unequivocally answer your prayer with a child, but I *am* saying that if you seek God He will always be gracious in responding. The Lord drew me out of the depths and rescued me from deep waters. I was dead in my suffering and He made me alive. He heard my prayer and He will hear yours too, Friend. "Because your *heart* was responsive and you humbled yourself before God when you heard what He spoke against this place and its people, and because you humbled yourself before me and tore your robes and wept in my presence, I have *heard* you, declares the Lord." (2 Chronicles 34:27)

Dear Lord,

Because you have encouraged me to pray, I will do so willingly. I pray out of my deepest longings for a child that you would be merciful in granting me one here on earth. "I will make rivers flow on barren heights, and springs within the valleys. I will turn the desert into pools of water, and the parched ground into springs." (Isaiah 41:18) Jesus, my comfort in suffering is that your promise preserves my life. (Psalms 119:50)

In Jesus' Name, Amen.

Week Three: *Pray for your future Child/Children.*

Day 19

GRACE

"For you formed my inward parts; you knitted me together
in my mother's womb. I praise you, for I am fearfully and
wonderfully made. Wonderful are your works; my soul knows
it very well. My frame was not hidden from you, when I
was being made in secret, intricately woven in the depths of
the earth. Your eyes saw my unformed substance; in your
book were written, every one of them, the days that were
formed for me, when as yet there was none of them."
Psalms 139:13-16 ESV

Infertility is a tangled web of tricky emotions. It's the stabbing
heartbreak when your best friend just told you she's pregnant—
taking everything within you to force a smile and hug her quickly
so she doesn't see the single tear slip down your cheek. It's crying
in the car on your lunch break. It's the shame of knowing your
husband was born to be a dad and you can't give him a child. It's the
exasperation of fighting insurance daily. It's feeling misunderstood.
It's experiencing gut-wrenching delays on a tightly timed cycle due
to a silly office mishap. It's peeing on a pregnancy test and tucking
it in your bathroom drawer to look at a few hours later just in case
the initial reading was wrong. It's dealing with PTSD and newfound

depression and absorbing the unintentionally hurtful comments. It's wondering if God really does care about you.

Infertility is a lot of things, touching every facet of life. But one thing I had not anticipated with this journey was all the sticky, web-like moral decisions that would go along with our infertility treatments: IUI, IVF, ICSI, PGS testing, assisted hatching, and the list goes on. Excess embryos: do you donate them to science, donate to another couple, destroy them once you're completed, or let them exist in an infinite frozen state? Being overwhelmed is an understatement. Additionally, since no one talks about this process, or at least no one I knew did, how are you supposed to get wise Godly counsel? Let me say this loud and clear: IVF, in particular, is not a morally black and white issue. By that statement, I am not making claims to what is right or what is wrong. But I am simply making the point that for anyone to make sweeping, definitive claims about infertility treatments since it is not explicitly addressed in the Bible is dangerously misguided. As a Christian, it was incredibly confusing when biblical opinions were presented as resolute moral certainty. I feel like a lack of understanding and ignorance by those shouting the loudest foster an environment of shame and secrecy for those hurting the deepest. Like unsuspecting insects in a spider's snare rolling deeper and deeper in the jaws of entrapment, I likewise was quickly entombed in this moral web of immobilizing guilt. And that's exactly how I felt—trapped. Let's look at God's Word for ourselves to see what He does say about conception:

> *Thus says the Lord who made you, who formed you from the womb and will help you: Fear not, O Jacob my servant, Jeshurun whom I have chosen.*
>
> —Isaiah 44:2 ESV

Did not he who made me in the womb make him? And did not one fashion us in the womb?

—Job 31:15 ESV

Behold, children are a heritage from the Lord, the fruit of the womb a reward.

—Psalms 127:3 ESV

I think we can all agree, based on scripture, once an embryo is placed inside the mother's womb, it is then up to our gracious Heavenly Father as to whether or not it results in a child and nothing should be done to harm or block the potential pregnancy. As my husband and I dug deeper into understanding the logistical and moral issues surrounding IVF and the resulting possibility of excess embryos, what we discovered in our search was that the vast majority of the "information" out there was purely people's opinion and surprisingly most of the time from individuals who admittedly had never personally dealt with the pain of infertility or even had to think about pursuing IVF. As Christians, we are caught between this emotional rock and a hard place of desperately wanting a child while simultaneously wrestling with our own personal convictions of where our moral "line in the sand" is drawn. There is this inner struggle of science and ethics and religion and desperation that all play into an already highly emotionally charged situation. Like spinning around ten times and running through an active minefield in snowshoes two sizes too big, our efforts in crowd-pleasing were doomed from the start. Halfway through our own cycle of IVF, my husband panicked and wanted to try to get as few embryos as possible, worrying that we were not going to make the right decision. It was at this low point a childhood friend of my husband who is a godly man and had previously gone through IVF called and gave us the advice we so desperately needed to hear. He gave us grace!

I would encourage you this—shut out the noise and the guilt and sit down with your Heavenly Father. Ask Him to convict your heart with what *you* believe is right and where you stand with the sanctity of life outside of the womb. Seek also the wise counsel from other godly couples who have been through this journey. I'm telling you this from the other side of infertility and with the clarity of hindsight: I would do IVF a thousand times over to have my sweet, precious, God-ordained Selah James. Please, do not let unfounded guilt rob you of potentially one of the greatest experiences of your life. I truly get emotional hearing different women's stories about the exquisite way in which their children were conceived—IUI, IVF, adoption, surrogacy. The intricate beauty each story of redemption holds always overwhelms me. So today, remember to embrace the beauty your unique journey holds. Allow God's grace to cover you and be encouraged.

Further reading for the sanctity of life in the womb:

Psalm 139:13-16
Luke 1:44
Psalm 22:9-10

Dear Lord,

"O Lord, you have searched me and known me! You know when I sit down and when I rise up; you discern my thoughts from afar. You search out my path and my lying down and are acquainted with all my ways. Even before a word is on my tongue, behold, O Lord, you know it altogether. You hem me in, behind and before, and lay your hand upon me." (Psalm 139:1-4 ESV) Lord, you already know the difficulties I face and that I desire to do the right thing. Give me certainty within my decision-making and cover me in your grace.

In Jesus' name, Amen.

Week Three: *Pray for your future Child/Children.*

Day 20

IDENTITY

"While walking by the Sea of Galilee, he [Jesus] saw two brothers, Simon (who is called Peter) and Andrew his brother, casting a net into the sea, for they were fishermen. And he said to them, 'Follow me, and I will make you fishers of men.' Immediately they left their nets and followed him. And going on from there he saw two other brothers, James the son of Zebedee and John his brother, in the boat with Zebedee their father, mending their nets, and he called them. Immediately they left the boat and their father and followed him."
Matthew 4:18-22 ESV

"But Ruth said, 'Do not urge me to leave you or to return from following you. For where you go I will go, and where you lodge I will lodge. Your people shall be my people, and your God my God. Where you die I will die, and there will I be buried. May the Lord do so to me and more also if anything but death parts me from you.' And when Naomi saw that she was determined to go with her, she said no more."
Ruth 1:16-18 ESV

Like delicate porcelain china dropping on the cold hard reality of a cement sidewalk, so my identity similarly shattered over and over with every unsuccessful cycle as the long-assumed label of "Mother" culminated into a whisper fine dust. We are taught from an early age that our performance, our successes, and people's perception of us contribute to our overall identity. The better we do in school, the more money we make as adults, and the more powerful or popular we become contributes to an overall more likable, more loved, and more accepted you. Culture praises perfection and applauds your successes. After years of this subtle indoctrination, we wholeheartedly believe that this success we achieve and how we are perceived give us purpose, assurance, and certainty as to who we are. The devil wants you so dependent on these things that when failure hits, when disappointment invades, and rejection permeates—like the porcelain china on cement—you are absolutely crushed.

The hardest part about the failure I experienced was that I seemed to stand still as everyone steadily passed me by. I was standing on a train platform watching window after window of happy families on the moving train of life grow smaller and smaller into the glowing horizon and the only thing matching my feelings of inadequacy was the worry I would never be able to catch up. My seemingly sub-par performance as a female led me to question my legitimacy to womanhood. I suddenly despised the broken body that was not able to perform the most basic function every woman was surely created for; and I felt like a fraud in every sense of the word. My body betrayed me and a crisis of identity ensued. When our identity is not fundamentally centered on the foundation of Christ, devastation of self is guaranteed. Likewise, if we base our ability to determine our self-worth on external and unreliable variables, then when failure at work emerges or our spouse leaves or our body cannot produce the child we so desperately want—the perception of our core purpose becomes problematic.

Rewiring our brain to fully embrace our identity in Christ is a slow and tedious process with the cultural brainwashing of self-reliance.

The stories of Peter and Ruth have beautiful similarities interwoven between the two. In their unhindered pursuit of Christ, they both rejected the security of worldly status to place their hope in something greater than themselves. Ruth left her ability to marry again, her hometown, and the protection of her family to honor and follow her mother-in-law and, ultimately, the new God she believed in. Peter left the family business and, like Ruth, chose to forgo societal pressures to follow Jesus. It is in this abandonment of self that authentic and unshakable identity is realized, not in the labels this world offers—or even the ones our souls long for—but solely Child of God.

A crisis of identity within infertility can shake us to our core and cause us to feel unsure of who we are and what we thought we would become. Like a bad dream in which you can't seem to move your feet or run away, the challenge of barrenness forces us to look our true identity square in the face, not the façade of elusive success or performance, but our actual character. The wounds we wear when looked at through the lens of Jesus have an innate ability to produce the very opposite of what we felt while struggling: namely, hope. Suffering cuts deep and we are so relieved when it's over, but there must be more than just the ugliness it renders. Our brokenness shapes us to where the scars we receive become the uniqueness we bear. Adversity can change our identities so profoundly that returning to our former selves would be preposterous, like a butterfly yearning to return to his caterpillar cocoon. You cannot talk about yourself and deny the intense struggle you have endured.

I was asked to introduce myself to a few new members in our Bible study recently, and in hindsight, my response struck me greatly. It went like this: "Hi, I'm Whitney. Married my college sweetheart, an infertility survivor with two miracle children, and I love traveling and horseback riding." My wounds have become some of the very first things I talk about. It has changed my identity in such a profound way that I refuse to let my past sufferings overtake my current strivings. Our day-to-day faith needs to reflect the identity we find in knowing Christ and if we allow Satan to riddle us with lies that we are not worthy, we surrender our ability to walk in the power and confidence He provides. I want to prepare you that you are going to emerge from this barren wilderness a different person with a new identity, and perhaps, at the end of the day, that's what the wilderness is all about. Regardless of your child-bearing abilities, you are a beautifully created woman of God made perfect by the scars you carry.

Dear Lord,

Help me to live in the power and confidence that you give daily, for it is no longer I who live but Christ who lives in me. (Galatians 2:20) Give me confidence in my self-worth regardless of the ever-changing and elusive external sources I desire to cling to.

In Jesus' name, Amen.

Week Three: *Pray for your future Child/Children.*

Day 21

HEALING

"When he [Jesus] saw them he said to them, "Go and show yourselves to the priests." And as they went they were cleansed. Then one of them, when he saw that he was healed, turned back, praising God with a loud voice; and he fell on his face at Jesus' feet, giving him thanks. Now he was a Samaritan. Then Jesus answered, "Were not ten cleansed? Where are the nine? Was no one found to return and give praise to God except this foreigner?" And he said to him, "Rise and go your way; your faith has made you well.""
Luke 17:14-19 ESV

I don't know the depths you've traveled to, the suffering you've endured, or the heartbreak you carry. For many of you reading this book, I probably cannot even begin to comprehend the losses you have suffered or the length in which you have been trudging through this valley. I know you are exhausted; but Friend, there will come a day where your heartbreak will not be palpable with every breath that you take. One day time will heal, wounds will mend, and scars will fade. Unfortunately, some stories of loss won't get the intellectual satisfaction of an earthy "why." They will remain a mystery as we sojourn on in this broken world. But there does come a point at which we arrive in our faith journey where we can confidently say, suffering is *never* for nothing and beauty from ashes flourishes in new ways.

I cannot guarantee there is a happy ending at the end of your journey, or at least the one that you envisioned for yourself, but I *can* guarantee that one day you will undoubtedly be on the other side of this barren valley. I *can* promise you wholeheartedly the Lord is going to show up in miraculous ways throughout your story, whether it's the testimony of how you suffered well and glorified Christ through your loss, the selfless love of a foster mom, the strength of embracing a childless life, or the birth of your own biological baby. When He does, and I'm telling you He will, never forget His faithfulness! Mark it down, shout it out, share your story, and remember always the one man that returned to Jesus in Luke 17. Let it be so of you because the Lord does not waste pain. "You intended to harm me, but God intended it for good to accomplish what is now being done, the saving of many lives." (Genesis 50:20) What was meant for your destruction might be the very thing God uses for your redemption. And if you think about it really, there is no power in redemption without the pain of suffering first. Your beautifully broken story might be the very thing that saves lives, provides comfort, and gives perspective to those who desperately need to hear it most.

In our household, one of the most precious stories of God's faithfulness is when the Lord dried up the Jordan so Joshua and the Israelites could cross on dry ground to take the Promised Land—the land of milk and honey—after wandering 40 years in the wilderness of waiting. In response to this miracle, Joshua set up a stone monument so the generations to come would be reminded of God's mighty faithfulness. We recount this story often and have many "Stones of Joshua" along the way in our marriage.

So Joshua called together the twelve men he had appointed from the Israelites, one from each tribe, and said to them, "Go over before the ark of the Lord your God into the middle of the Jordan. Each of you is to take up a stone on his shoulder, according to the number of the tribes of the Israelites, to serve as a sign among you. In the future, when your children ask you, 'What do these stones mean?' tell them that the flow of the Jordan was cut off before the ark of the covenant of the Lord. When it crossed the Jordan, the waters of the Jordan were cut off. These stones are to be a memorial to the people of Israel forever."

—Joshua 4:4-7

We named our son Stone to forever memorialize the hard-fought battle in our barren wilderness and the miraculous ways in which God works. Christmas 2017, two days before my pre-op appointment for Frozen Embryo Transfer #2, I shockingly found out I was pregnant naturally. We not only celebrated the birth of our savior that holiday, God's only son, but the conception of new life as well—our son. He is truly our Stone of Joshua—a walking reminder of God's timing, not ours. I will always be the one man that returns. I will always find my way back to the feet of Jesus and forever proclaim His faithfulness. My barren cry is now my song of redemption. So, for those of you who have been healed from your affliction, may you never lose sight of the *mighty* things God has done. For those still waiting for healing, have hope and do not lose heart, as your story is not yet finished. "For He who is mighty has done great things for me, and HOLY is His name." (Luke 1:49 ESV)

Hannah's Prayer:

"Then Hannah prayed and said: 'My heart rejoices in the Lord; in the Lord my horn is lifted high. My mouth boasts over my enemies, for I delight in your deliverance. There is no one holy like the Lord; there is no one besides you; there is no Rock like our God. Do not keep talking so proudly or let your mouth speak such arrogance, for the Lord is a God who knows, and by him deeds are weighed. The bows of the warriors are broken, but those who stumbled are armed with strength. Those who were full hire themselves out for food, but those who were hungry are hungry no more. She who was barren has borne seven children, but she who has had many sons pines away. The Lord brings death and makes alive; he brings down to the grave and raises up. The Lord sends poverty and wealth; he humbles and he exalts. He raises the poor from the dust and lifts the needy from the ash heap; he seats them with princes and has them inherit a throne of honor. For the foundations of the earth are the Lord's on them he has set the world. He will guard the feet of his faithful servants, but the wicked will be silenced in the place of darkness. It is not by strength that one prevails; those who oppose the Lord will be broken. The Most High will thunder from heaven; the Lord will judge the ends of the earth. He will give strength to his king and exalt the horn of his anointed.'" (1 Samuel 2:1-10)

In Jesus' name, Amen.

Week Three: *Pray for your future Child/Children.*

Epilogue

Dear Friend,

I hope you have been challenged, encouraged, and felt loved on these past three weeks. It has been my absolute joy and privilege to have journeyed with you, if not just for a short while. Thank you for opening your heart and mind to the things the Lord has impressed upon me to share. I pray you would continue on with assured hope that your miracle is just around the corner. If you are silently struggling and need more help, visit www.whitneyhenneman.com to locate additional resources and support.

If your suffering has awakened a cavernous void of unfulfillment and hopelessness, I am confident the only thing that satisfies the intense yearning you feel is a relationship with Jesus Christ. If you are new to this whole God thing, don't worry! There is nothing in the world that offers a plan of hope, redemption, and eternal life at the cost of *nothing* to you. It doesn't matter who you are, what you've done, or how you've come. God wants to meet you exactly where you are and loves all of you—the good, the bad, and the ugly. Jesus came specifically to save the lost, comfort the hurting, and redeem the oppressed. Salvation through Jesus doesn't require a subscription to religion, tithing, a set of strict rules, sacraments, self-power, or sacrifices—just a heart of confession and a mind of belief. Believing in Jesus, as I've written throughout this book, does not mean the circumstances of your life will necessarily get easier, but it does guarantee the heavy load you carry will become bearable by discovering true joy, transcendent peace, and lasting contentment. "Come to me [Jesus], all you who are weary and burdened, and I will give you rest. Take my yoke upon you and learn from me, for I am gentle and humble in heart, and you will find rest for your souls. For my yoke is easy and my burden is light." (Matthew 11:28-30)

The Bible lays the plan of salvation like this:

> *for all have sinned and fall short of the glory of God, and are justified by his grace as a gift, through the redemption that is in Christ Jesus,*
>
> —Romans 3:23-24 ESV

> *For the wages of sin is death, but the gift of God is eternal life in Christ Jesus our Lord.*
>
> —Romans 6:23

God, in His great love for us, sent his one and only son to die on a cross as atonement for our sins so that we might be rectified with Him.

> *For God so loved the world that he gave his one and only Son, that whoever believes in him shall not perish but have eternal life.*
>
> —John 3:16

> *But God demonstrates his own love for us in this: While we were still sinners, Christ died for us.*
>
> —Romans 5:8

Our response to God's great sacrifice is to believe with our hearts and confess with our mouths that Jesus is Lord.

If you declare with your mouth, 'Jesus is Lord,' and believe in your heart that God raised him from the dead, you will be saved. For it is with your heart that you believe and are justified, and it is with your mouth that you profess your faith and are saved.

—Romans 10:9-10

Very truly I tell you, whoever hears my word and believes him who sent me has eternal life and will not be judged but has crossed over from death to life.

—John 5:24

Through this confession of faith, we will receive the Holy Spirit and be granted eternal life in Heaven with God.

And this is the testimony: God has given us eternal life, and this life is in his Son. Whoever has the Son has life; whoever does not have the Son of God does not have life.

—1 John 5:11-12 NIV

If you feel God calling to you today, pray this simple prayer of faith with me:

Dear Jesus,

I recognize that I am a sinner so, please, forgive me for my sins and cleanse me of all unrighteousness. I declare with my mouth that Jesus is Lord and believe in my heart that God raised him from the dead. (Romans 10:9) Create in me a pure heart and renew a steadfast spirit within me. (Psalm 51:10) Thank you for everlasting and unshakeable hope in you despite the crushing suffering I have endured. Allow the peace of God, which surpasses all understanding, to guard my heart and mind in Christ Jesus. (Philippians 4) Amen!

Welcome to the family, my new Sister in Christ! The Bible tells us angels are rejoicing over *you* in Heaven. "In the same way, I tell you, there is rejoicing in the presence of the angels of God over one sinner who repents." (Luke 15:10) I would encourage you to reach out to a local Bible-believing church for the next steps in growing your faith and finding a community of believers that will support you in this exciting new journey you have begun.

Acknowledgments

To my husband **Lane**, You are the roots to my leaves and the string to my kite. You are my grounding force, my biggest cheerleader, and my greatest love. As we have journeyed through this life hand in hand, we have seen the highest mountaintops and the deepest valleys. There is no greater feeling on this earth than to be fully known and truly seen. Your love is life to me. Thank you for always encouraging me to share our story.

To my editor, **Tanya Cramer**, thank you for graciously lending your time and expertise in allowing this project to come to life. Your encouragement means more than you know.

Selah and Stone, my two precious miracles who fill my life with immeasurable joy, I want you to know as profound as the suffering was that we endured to conceive you, I would do it a million times over to hold you in my arms once again. Your love, your smell, your giggles, and your innocence have allowed me to truly taste the *best* this life has to offer.

Finally, I want to give love to all my **infertility besties**, near and far, who trudged with me in the thick of it—who have known the tears I cried, understood the bitterness I felt, and processed their journey alongside me. You are always near to my heart.

Endnotes

1   C.S. Lewis, *The Problem of Pain* (New York: Harper Collins, 2001), page 16.

2   "What Does It Mean That God Is Sovereign?" Got Questions, 2020, https://www.gotquestions.org/God-is-sovereign.html.

3   J. Boivin, E. Griffiths, and C.A. Venetis, "Emotional Distress in Infertile Women and Failure of Assisted Reproductive Technologies: Meta-Analysis of Prospective Psychosocial Studies." *BMJ*, 342 (2011): d223.

4   Elisabeth Elliot, *Suffering Is Never for Nothing* (Nashville: B&H Publishing Group, 2019), page 83.

5   Jerry L. Sittser, *A Grace Disguised: How the Soul Grows through Loss* (Grand Rapids: Zondervan, 1995), page 45.

6   Charles H. Spurgeon, *Strengthen My Spirit* (Uhrichsville: Barbour Publishing, 2011), Kindle edition, location 782-801.

7   C.S. Lewis, *The Problem of Pain* (New York: Harper Collins, 2001), page 91.

8   Toby Mac (@tobymac), "My wife and I would want the world to know this…," *Instagram*, October 24, 2019, https://www.instagram.com/p/B4BBfFcBeMg/ ?igshid=nhzb36hjuu91.

9   *The Usual Suspects*, directed by Bryan Singer (1995; Universal City, CA: Gramercy Pictures, 1995), YouTube.

10 *The Chronicles of Narnia: The Voyage of the Dawn Treader*, directed by Michael Apted (2010; Los Angeles, CA: 20th Century Fox, 2010), Amazon.

11 "Quotes Misattributed to C.S. Lewis," C.S. Lewis Foundation, 2020, http://www.cslewis.org/aboutus/faq/quotes-misattributed/.